Introduction to social security

Introduction to social security

International Labour Office   Geneva

ISBN 92-2-103638-3

First published 1958
Second edition 1970
Third edition 1984

Printed in Switzerland

PREFACE

This handbook is the direct successor of the ILO manual which in 1958 presented the subject of social security in a series of ten lessons, and went through five successive impressions before being revised and enlarged in 1970 to take account of changes in those 12 years. The fact that the text has now had to be completely revised and largely rewritten demonstrates not only that the material has outgrown the original framework but also how social security itself is an evolving concept, responding to new situations, moving into fresh areas of the world, and adapting its ways to new fields of administration.

As the subject-matter extends and diversifies, its treatment in a publication like this necessarily changes. The attempt to be exhaustive has to be resisted, as has the temptation to be superficial and to describe in too general terms matters which closely touch the lives of so many people, be they workers, heads of families, pensioners or citizens. The present volume aims at a middle course. It is intended to be an introduction to social security for the ordinary reader who looks for a reasonably complete explanation of what the subject is all about and it will, when taken together with other material available from the ILO and from the authorities which administer national programmes of social security, provide a basis for courses of study in adult and workers' educational groups and other bodies interested in aspects of social welfare and civic affairs. For the student who wishes to pursue the subject, or some aspect of it, in greater depth and detail, there are some suggestions for further reading at the end of the volume.

Social security is, as these chapters bear witness, one side of a coin. Positive action to promote employment, personal and public health, safety at places of work and the well-being of mothers and children may be deemed to be of greater importance. But the services which come to the aid of workers when their wages are interrupted by sickness or injury, which enable expectant or nursing mothers to suspend their work, which support invalids and orphans and which provide an income in old age and widowhood, are no less important to the community, together with the security that resides in the knowledge that they will be there if and whenever they are needed.

CONTENTS

List of Tables

SOCIAL SECURITY 1

THE HISTORICAL PROBLEM

During the nineteenth century, countries which are now regarded as "industrialised nations" first began to emerge from the throes of the industrial revolution, which transformed the face of Europe and was a major part of the formative history of North America. Such countries had to cope with the social and economic results of that experience. The other countries of the world were moving, at first tentatively and then at an accelerated pace, to match the commercial and industrial developments of their neighbours. The process threw up problems of many kinds, none more obvious than the sight of poverty amongst plenty, of need amidst unused resources, of destitution on the sidewalks of riches.

Long before any formal recognition of the need for community action, the relief of poverty had been commended as a private obligation. Religious foundations provided shelter, sanctuary and alms; mediaeval trade guilds supported members and their families in times of adversity. Out of these beginnings, some countries developed systems of poor law to relieve and accommodate the destitute, laws which had the merit of admitting public liability, while establishing the principle of using public money for the purpose, and of being comprehensive in their scope. But being designed, as some would say, to minimise the likelihood of social unrest in reaction to actual starvation, these laws did little more than blunt the edge of the problem. Nothing was paid until the applicant had exhausted all personal resources and failed to get help from relatives. No one was likely to accept the humiliation of poor law relief (which could involve loss of civil rights, and compulsory removal, of husband and wife separately, to the poor-house) if that could possibly be avoided. In countries outside the money economy, the traditional bulwark against poverty was the support of the family, or the extended family of clan and tribal village, with each generation accepting the duty of caring for the elderly and for the weaker brethren. But with intensive industrialisation on the one hand, there was a gradual move away from pastoral and subsistence economies on the other, and these various forms of protection,

1

rooted in history and tradition, became progressively less adequate to meet the new situation.

ALTERNATIVE REMEDIES

As the pace of industrialisation quickened, a large new class of factory workers emerged, completely dependent for their livelihood on the regular payment of wages. They could well be reduced to privation if and when their wages stopped during sickness and unemployment, following work injury or in old age. In the attempt to protect the urban labouring classes from destitution, several other systems evolved. There were, for instance, savings bank facilities sponsored by government; there were measures laying upon employers some obligation to maintain the ill or injured workman; there was the growth of mutual aid societies organised to provide modest cash aid in sickness and old age; and private insurance developed simple life policies and funeral benefits.

All this went a certain, though only a limited, way towards meeting the problem. For a main social error of the time was the persistence of the optimistic belief that, if workers were left to themselves, they would be willing and able and imaginative enough to cover their risks individually or under some voluntary collective arrangement. The error should have been obvious enough. Workers were totally absorbed in survival from one day to the next, and hardly had time to consider distant eventualities. Meeting the certain expenses of today took precedence over saving for the possibilities of tomorrow. Nor was there anything to spare against the more immediate risks of sickness or unemployment. Yet, at the same time, with the spread of education and the widening of the franchise, there was an awakening of hope and an expectation of better things to come, for future generations if not in the present. Gradually, social and political pressure groups made their influence felt at policy-making levels. Some countries reacted faster than others, and the process was given an extra impetus after the major world crises — during the reconstruction periods following the First and Second World Wars, and during the period of action against the economic depression of the early thirties.

Piece by piece, like a jigsaw puzzle waiting to emerge, separate benefit programmes were assembled until, in the industrialised countries, the coverage established was virtually total, both as to population groups and as to the various contingencies which threaten the wages and income, and thus the quality and standard of living, of working people. And the new term "social security" was found to describe this new state of affairs.

SOCIAL SECURITY: A DEFINITION

This necessarily brief summary traces the development of the concept which has come to be known as social security. The expression has acquired a wider interpretation in some countries than in others, but basically it can be taken to mean the protection which society provides for its members, through a series of public measures, against the economic and social distress that otherwise would be caused by the stoppage or substantial reduction of earnings resulting from sickness, maternity, employment injury, unemployment, invalidity, old age and death; the provision of medical care; and the provision of subsidies for families with children.

The term "social security" was first officially used in the title of the United States legislation — the Social Security Act of 1935 — even though this Act initiated programmes to meet the risks of old age, death, disability and unemployment only. It appeared again in an Act passed in New Zealand in 1938 which brought together a number of existing and new social security benefits. It was used in 1941 in the wartime document known as the Atlantic Charter. The ILO was quick to adopt the term, impressed by its value as a simple and arresting expression of one of the deepest and most widespread aspirations of people all around the world.

The following paragraphs recapitulate the various strands which have come together in comprehensive social security as we know it today, and note briefly the formal action taken by the ILO between 1952 and 1982 to codify the concept. These strands are: social insurance; social assistance; benefits financed by general revenue; family benefits; and provident funds, together with supplementary provisions made by employers, and the ancillary and complementary programmes which have developed around social security.

SOCIAL INSURANCE

The first broad system of social insurance was created by the Government of Germany under Chancellor Bismarck between 1883 and 1889, though as far back as the 1850s several German states had helped local governments to set up sickness funds to which workmen could be compelled to contribute. The principle of compulsory insurance was thus already being applied, although at this stage the sole contributor was the insured person. Sickness insurance, which began in 1883 and was managed by existing mutual aid funds, was the first stage. Employment injury insurance, operated by employers' trade associations, came in 1884. Invalidity and old-age insurance, administered by the provinces, followed in 1889. Already all three of the social partners — workers, employers and the State — were playing their part and had a voice in the management of the scheme as a whole. Social insurance, as the name implies, was financed by contributions. It was compulsory for the wage earners for whom it was designed: employees, skilled and unskilled alike, young and elderly, male and female, and regardless of their state of health. Now all these people, who had had little to fall back on but the Poor Law, were protected by a system of guaranteed benefits, out of the shadow of the means test and the poor-house. The insurance principle gave expression to the solidarity of the workers — each contributing regularly to support colleagues and workmates in the time of their need — and to the interest of both sides of industry in financing a scheme whose results would be beneficial not only to the workforce but also to the management.

The example of Germany was followed in Europe and elsewhere, and by the 1930s social insurance had spread to Latin America, the United States and Canada. Following the achievement of national independence and at different times after the end of the Second World War, social insurance was introduced in many countries in Africa, Asia and the Caribbean area.

There are differences between one scheme and another but the principal elements of social insurance may be set out as follows:

— social insurance is financed by contributions which are normally shared between employers and workers, with, perhaps, state participation in the form of a supplementary contribution or other subsidy from the general revenue;

— participation is compulsory, with few exceptions;

— contributions are accumulated in special funds out of which benefits are paid;

— surplus funds not needed to pay current benefits are invested to earn further income;

— a person's right to benefit is secured by his contribution record without any test of need or means;

— contribution and benefit rates are often related to what the person is or has been earning;

— employment injury insurance schemes are usually financed wholly by employers, with the possibility of state help from general revenue.

SOCIAL ASSISTANCE

Some countries, mainly those in Scandinavia, started their social security systems with programmes of what is now called social assistance, financed from the general revenue of the country rather than from individual contributions, with statutory scales of benefit adjusted according to a person's means. The first group of people to be covered in this way were the elderly, then the sick, invalids, survivors and the unemployed, respectively. In time, state provision through social assistance (which might be characterised as a liberalised version of Poor Law, financed and administered by the central Government) has usually been superseded by contributory social insurance, but in some countries, for example Australia and New Zealand, complete social security systems have been constructed by the amalgamation of a series of social assistance schemes.

Even in countries which rely in the main upon social insurance, a type of social assistance may be available as a "safety net" for those persons who in one way or another fall outside the scope of the main scheme, or whose insurance benefit is insufficient to meet their need.

The principal features of social assistance may be described as follows:

— the whole cost of the programme is met by the State and local units of government;

— benefits are paid as of legal right in prescribed categories of need;

— in assessing need, a person's other income and resources are taken into account; certain resources, such as a reasonable level of personal savings, are disregarded;

— the benefit grant is designed to bring a person's total income up to a community-determined minimum, taking into account other factors such as family size and unavoidable fixed obligations such as rent; grants are not related to the applicant's previous earnings or customary standard of living;

— social assistance has certain affinities with social welfare case work, as it is problem-oriented and, unlike social insurance, gives a certain amount of scope for discretion in determining awards, provided that such discretion is exercised within the framework of the rights established under the law.

BENEFITS FINANCED BY GENERAL REVENUE

Yet another route to social security has been chosen by a number of countries. This is the direct provision by the State, wholly or largely from general revenue, of standard benefits to each resident in a specified category. These benefits may include a pension to every aged, invalid, orphaned or widowed resident. Similarly, some countries operate a national health service providing medical care for all without a contribution or means test; the cost may be met wholly or mainly from public funds, although there may be partial charges for dental, ophthalmic or other specialist services — charges which may be remitted for specified classes of beneficiaries.

FAMILY BENEFITS

Family benefits occupy a place of their own in the development of social security. While a certain analogy can be drawn between sickness benefit and maternity benefit, the continued expense of raising a family has not always been viewed as a contingency against which the individual or the community should be protected through social insurance. However, it is perhaps arguable that the provision of a fund financed by employers for the benefit of the families of wage earners is a form of insurance. A fuller survey of family benefits will be found in Chapter 11.

PROVIDENT FUNDS

A number of developing countries which entered the field of comprehensive social security at a later date and which sought, as they saw it, simplicity of administration decided to establish state provident funds. A provident fund is a means of compulsory saving. Workers and their employers pay regular contributions into a central fund and the contributions are credited to a separate account, to which interest is added periodically, for each worker. When specified events occur, such as old age, invalidity or death, the total standing to the credit of the account is paid out to the worker or to the survivors. Some funds permit earlier partial withdrawals in the event of sickness or unemployment or for other stated purposes such as house purchase.

By introducing the practice of regular saving towards certain (or, in some circumstances, uncertain) future occasions of need, provident funds have played a valuable part in promoting the idea of self-help, and there is no doubt that a lump-sum benefit, wisely expended, can be particularly valuable, say at the point of retirement. On the other hand, it can be said that a provident fund is not a social security scheme in the conventional sense: it is not geared to provide periodical payment in lieu of wages which cease on retirement from regular employment or are lost through invalidity. A provident fund benefit is in part a terminal bonus, in part deferred pay, with little relevance to age or to the circumstances in which the employment ends. Nor is there any pooling of risk among the covered group of workers. In an inflationary situation, contributions lose much of their purchasing power before they ultimately emerge as benefit. For these reasons, it is not surprising that those who launched provident funds invariably stated their intention to transform them into social insurance funds in due course. Such a transformation is not the straightforward operation which it might seem, and it does appear in practice that, in simplicity of operation, there is little to choose between a provident fund and an insurance scheme — if anything, the balance of advantage lies with the latter.

PROVISION MADE BY EMPLOYERS

Employers' liability schemes came into being towards the end of the nineteenth century and were mainly directed towards the risk of employment injury. Many such schemes still exist in developed and developing countries alike. They place legal responsibility on the employer to provide compensation and medical care in respect of employment injuries, and to do so either directly or under an approved insurance policy. When the employer does insure, the policy will sometimes go beyond the statutory liability under the compensation scheme and will protect the worker's rights if the employer should become liable to pay damages under the general law.

The scope and extent of provision by employers has, however, widened considerably over the years. Some national legislation requires the grant of paid sick leave for so many days of absence in a year or for the first few weeks of sickness, and similarly the grant of paid maternity leave (indeed, in some countries these benefits were introduced before employment injury benefits). There are labour laws which give workers the right to severance or redundancy payments on dismissal and to medical care for themselves, and sometimes for their families, at the employer's expense. Such arrangements may be found even where there is no statutory obligation: it is a fruitful area for collective industrial agreements.

What has become especially significant is the increasing variety of occupational pension plans which are created by employers for their own staff and which provide pensions in addition to, or in partial substitution of, the state social security pension. Although non-statutory in form, and often specially tailored to suit the personnel policy of the employer concerned, such schemes are normally constructed to fit in with the state pension scheme and may enjoy official encouragement through tax concessions.

SOCIAL SERVICES

As the preface to this book has indicated, social security cash benefits and social services can be regarded as two sides of one coin. They have everywhere grown up together and the policy imperatives which dictate the one dictate the other. Any inventory of relevant social services would include health services; preventive action in health care and against accidents; rehabilitation of the injured; special facilities for the disabled and old people; child welfare and care; family planning clinics — the list would be long. Health services have been touched upon earlier, and the extent to which any of these services is integrated with social security at the policy level, at the level of departmental and local administration, in shared premises or with common staffs, through linked financial arrangements or otherwise, depends upon such factors as the historic development of the social security system itself, the social and political organisation of the country, the extent and structure of the various programmes, and the priorities attached to their component parts.

7

INTERNATIONAL LABOUR CONVENTIONS

The ILO has played an important role in relation to social security development. The prime concern of the ILO is the formulation of international policies and programmes to improve working and living conditions. One of the principal ways in which it does this is through international labour Conventions, the drafting of which involves the ILO secretariat in extensive study and discussion, and in the examination of existing laws and practices throughout the world. A Convention is conceived as a set of firm criteria for the preparation of national legislation. When it has been adopted by the annual International Labour Conference, member States of the ILO are required by the Constitution to bring the Convention to the notice of their legislative authorities. In due course, if the standards which have been set are embodied in national laws, the States concerned will be in a position to ratify the Convention. Not every State which follows the Convention necessarily proceeds to ratification, but the influence of the ILO in setting standards is effective regardless of the formal procedures involved.

A landmark in international social security was the adoption by the International Labour Conference of the ILO on 28 June 1952 of the Social Security (Minimum Standards) Convention (No. 102). This brought together in one comprehensive document the policies to which the then member States were prepared to subscribe, and defined the range of benefits which form the core of social security. It laid down minimum requirements as to coverage of the population and the content and level of benefits, and covered the protection of the rights of contributors and beneficiaries and ancillary matters of administration.

In succeeding chapters, the Social Security (Minimum Standards) Convention, 1952 (No. 102), will be referred to frequently.

Convention No. 102 maintains its authority as setting important basic standards, even though, in the meantime, the ILO has moved on to a series of more detailed Conventions on specific branches of social security. These are listed below. Also listed are a number of "Recommendations". These are international instruments similar to Conventions but not subject to the formal processes of ratification. A Recommendation lays down detailed standards which it is desirable should be achieved, often on subjects for which a Convention was considered too rigid a procedure. Where a Convention is accompanied by a Recommendation, the latter will suggest certain lines of advance beyond the limits defined in the more mandatory Articles of the Convention.

Relevant Conventions and Recommendations

Social Security (Minimum Standards) Convention, 1952 (No. 102)
Maternity Protection Convention (Revised), 1952 (No. 103)

Maternity Protection Recommendation, 1952 (No. 95)

Equality of Treatment (Social Security) Convention, 1962 (No. 118) (concerning equality of treatment of nationals and non-nationals)

Employment Injury Benefits Convention, 1964 (No. 121)

Employment Injury Benefits Recommendation, 1964 (No. 121)

Invalidity, Old-Age and Survivors' Benefits Convention, 1967 (No. 128)

Invalidity, Old-Age and Survivors' Benefits Recommendation, 1967 (No. 131)

Medical Care and Sickness Benefits Convention, 1969 (No. 130)

Medical Care and Sickness Benefits Recommendation, 1969 (No. 134)

Older Workers Recommendation, 1980 (No. 162) (concerning equality of opportunity and treatment for older workers, their protection in employment, and preparation for and access to retirement)

Maintenance of Social Security Rights Convention, 1982 (No. 157)

Maintenance of Social Security Rights Recommendation, 1983 (No. 167)

THE SPREAD OF SOCIAL SECURITY

After the end of the Second World War, the number of countries operating some kind of social security programme rose sharply. Social security was an important part of any reconstruction effort, and a prime interest of newly emerging countries, more than 60 of whom achieved independence at this time. The figures in table 1 have been published by the Social Security Administration of the United States Department of Health and Human Services.

Table 1.   Number of countries with social security programmes throughout the world in 1949, 1967 and 1981 [1]

Programme	1949	1967	1981
Any type of programme	58	120	139
Old age, invalidity, survivors	44	92	127
Sickness and maternity	36	65	79
Employment injury	57	117	136
Unemployment	22	34	37
Family allowances	27	62	67

[1] A number of countries are not included in the table either because they had no social security programme or because data were lacking.

Source. United States Department of Health and Human Services, Social Security Administration: *Social security programs throughout the world, 1981*, Research Report, No. 58 (Washington, DC, Government Printing Office, 1981).

9

The most notable feature of the table is the importance attached to employment injury cover. No matter what other form of protection had been organised, nearly every country in the survey had some type of employment injury scheme: in some cases in the form of social insurance, in others by placing a legal liability on employers. Occasionally both techniques are found side by side in different sectors of employment, for example when the transition from an older system to social insurance is not yet complete.

Most countries have made provision for old age, invalidity and survivors, again in different ways through social insurance, social assistance, provident funds or general revenue-financed schemes for residents. More than one-half of them cover sickness and maternity, and about the same number supplement family resources through a regular system of allowances. Only about one-quarter of them provide unemployment benefit, which for the most part is found only in industrialised market-economy countries.

THE PERSONS PROTECTED 2

THE AIM IS TOTAL AND UNIFORM COVER

That social security should extend protection to the whole community is a truism. That its protection should be uniform for each section of the community is simple social justice. And that the whole community should stand together, non-national residents equally with national residents, to provide this protection is an expression of the solidarity which underlies the whole concept.

For good practical and historical reasons, those ideals of universal and uniform protection at the expense of the community at large result in a diversity of cover and a variety of emphasis over the whole field of social security benefits. Many industrial countries would contend that the general aim has been achieved and that all sectors of the community, wage earners, self-employed and non-employed alike, have been brought under the protection of social security in one way or another. Reliance is usually placed on a social insurance system, accompanied by schemes of family benefits, on social assistance, or on guaranteed pensions for residents. Statutory recognition may be given to occupational benefits provided by employers, by self-employed persons, or under industrial agreements; or these may be regarded, like commercial insurance, as a private voluntary extension of the state provision.

Even so, no country would claim to have completed and perfected its social security cover. Further improvements in benefits and services, the relaxation of qualifying conditions and the adjustment, or even withdrawal, of some aspect of benefit to match changing economic and social circumstances are always possible, and rightly so. Social security is pre-eminently an area in which social and political pressure groups each deploy their own arguments, and if a system is to be effective and to live up to its name, it should respond to new demands as they are placed on it by changes in working and living conditions — always provided that the response can be financed and does not distort the balance of the system.

Partial and uneven coverage often occurs during the period when a country is building up its social security programme. For a while there may be a patchwork of provisions, at worst piece-meal, at best in carefully planned phases each fitting neatly into the next until the whole pattern emerges. It is interesting to consider in greater detail why that pattern cannot be, and indeed in some respects ought not to be, even and uniform. Reasons can be found in the conventional layout of benefits and contingencies to be met; in the demands and compulsions of administrative procedures; in the different balance of economic activity from one country to another, or in different regions of the same country; and in the peculiarities of some major groups which have in the past produced special rules and exceptions. Even the search for uniformity of treatment may result in inequalities being built into the system.

THE CONVENTION PATTERN

Convention No. 102 analyses comprehensive social security under nine branches of benefit. The minimum level of coverage which it demands is moderate — in some branches not more than 50 per cent of the persons at risk — so that few countries would fail to meet the standard. More importantly, the Convention recognises that not all persons are even at risk in some branches, differentiating, for example, between unemployment and employment injury benefits which cover employed persons only, and other social insurance benefits which are appropriate to both the employed and the self-employed. Even within the main standards set by the Convention, a developing country whose "economy and medical facilities are insufficiently developed" may avail itself of temporary exceptions when applying for ratification. All these varying degrees of cover are spelled out in the Convention.

THE EFFECT OF ADMINISTRATIVE PROCEDURES

Identification

A contributory scheme of long-term benefits requires a basic numbering system which will separately identify each individual contributor and each contribution made by that contributor (or by the employer on the contributor's behalf). This system will enable the clerk in the social security headquarters, who has never met the individual, to recognise the contributor, and to credit these contributions to the correct account. The same identity system will ensure that, when the account is translated into a pension or other benefit, this will be paid to the correct person.

Thus, at the outset, the social security administration is confronted with a massive registration exercise, which must be carried through with absolute accuracy so that there is no confusion in the future. Because age is an important element in identification, the task is even more time-consuming in a country which does not have a well-established system of civil registration. Also, as it is desirable for the contribution records so created to be brought into use with the least delay, it is clear why the first registration must be concentrated on those members of the community who are most easily reached and for whom formal records are more likely to exist. Thus, coverage in a number of schemes will often be limited initially to larger employers, say with 100 or more employees, in order to cover a substantial proportion of the workforce, and the remaining proportion will be picked up in a later operation. Indeed, there are schemes which, despite a fairly lengthy period of operation, have not been extended beyond their initial coverage; thus, for example, employers of fewer than five workers, and workers in private domestic employment, have not been taken into account because of the high unit cost of collection through small employers as compared with large firms.

Casual workers form another category of employed persons who may be left out of any type of contributory scheme because of the difficulty of registering them and of keeping track of their movements. They are even difficult to define for the purpose of administration.

Concentration on the employed sector

Reliance upon the social insurance system as a method of financing a social security fund has the consequence that benefit cover tends to be limited to employed persons. One of the selling points of an insurance scheme is the value that it offers to the employee, whose contribution may be doubled by the employer and may attract a supplement from the State. A side-effect of this bargain is to discourage the compulsory, or even voluntary, coverage of self-employed persons, because the apparent cost of the contribution is nearly twice what the employed person has to pay. In addition, a country which has an appreciable number of self-employed persons — such as market women, small shopkeepers, agricultural smallholders, taxi drivers — may find it impossible to bring them within the social insurance net. Furthermore, when benefits are financed in this way, it is difficult to introduce the category of non-employed persons.

The compulsory inclusion of self-employed and non-employed persons in a state-wide contributory system of social security has always been an intractable problem because of the difficulty of enforcing compliance. This difficulty is compounded when contributions are assessed in proportion to earnings or income. One solution has been to make participation voluntary or, where the obligation is compulsory, to allow self-assessment for contributions with corresponding levels of benefit.

13

OTHER CAUSES OF UNEQUAL COVERAGE

Higher paid employees

In the early days of social security — and examples are still found in workmen's compensation legislation — it was the practice to exclude workers who were earning more than a stated rate of wage or salary, on the reasonable argument at the time that they were at less risk and could in any event obtain personal insurance. Later, with the evolution of general schemes of social security giving flat-rate benefits, the idea of universal coverage took root, but the inclusion of higher paid workers created another difficulty. A standard level of contribution for a standard rate of benefit, suitable for the middle range of wages of the workforce, resulted in a disproportionately high deduction from low wages on the one hand, and produced a benefit which in no way matched the need of the higher paid contributor on the other.

This was, of course, one of the reasons for the appearance of earnings-related systems of social security, with benefits graded according to the claimant's interrupted or lost earnings, and financed by a percentage levy on the earnings of covered contributors. However, where benefit is related to earnings, it is usual to find that a maximum rate of benefit is prescribed: this does not normally nowadays exclude highly paid employees from social security cover; it simply means that, beyond a certain level of remuneration, all beneficiaries qualify for the same maximum rate of benefit.

Occupational pension plans

The gradual and increasing growth of social security has been paralleled by the development of private pension plans, operated by or on behalf of employers for their own employees, by employees themselves, or by both sides of industry. This has given rise to the attractive idea that fuller provision for old age may be assured by a partnership between social security and occupational plans which produces the following:

(a) a state pension, flat-rate and/or earnings-related; and

(b) an occupational pension, privately financed.

Although there are certainly divided opinions on this issue, it has been argued that such a linking of public and private provision could reduce the extent to which the State need organise and finance old-age pensions. Some countries with highly developed programmes have devoted much study to creating links of this kind, but the subject is highly complex, with ramifications which would unduly extend this book.

Government and parastatal workers

In many countries, government workers were covered by comprehensive legislation for occupational benefits — sickness and maternity pay, retirement and survivors' pensions, accident provisions — before general social security programmes were embarked upon. Indeed, the very existence of public service pensions legislation was behind the moulding of public opinion in favour of social security protection for the rest of the community.

From one point of view, this legislation constitutes an occupational pension plan operated by the government as employer for the benefit of its own employees, and could be looked at in the same way as other plans, in relation to social security. This is not possible for a number of reasons. The provisions are often comprehensive over the whole field of employment risks (with the exception, perhaps, of premature termination of employment after short service). The rights to old-age, employment injury and invalidity benefits, and often survivors' benefits as well, are firmly secured by public legislation as a part of the conditions of service of the persons concerned. These benefits are often paid, like salaries, out of public funds, although there are instances where contributions are levied from the workers themselves. Often, general programmes of social security have exempted people who are included in this kind of coverage.

At the same time, the principle of solidarity is strong, not least in developing countries, in relation to universal and uniform provision under social security. Alterations in conditions of service and the preservation of acquired rights to benefit are proper matters for negotiation, and uniform coverage is being approached in different ways by successive steps.

Parastatal organisations, typical of which are statutory boards charged with the responsibility of operating public utilities, occupy an intermediate position between government and private employers. In so far as the organisation has been "hived off" from a government department, at least some of its employees may still be identified under government pensions Acts, while the remainder come naturally under the cover of the general social security programme. On the other hand, a statutory board which is set up wholly outside the existing public service would be covered by the social security programme on the same terms as any other employer.

Rural areas and agriculture

In all cases, the first measures of social security reflect the economic needs of the urban industrial community. Any extension of coverage to the agricultural community implies that schemes have to be introduced into a very different setting, and the type of need may in fact be very different from that of the urban wage earner.

There is no single, world-wide, uniform model of agricultural activity. Variations stem from all sorts of local conditions — tradition, soil, climate, systems of land tenure, communications, extent of industrialisation, level of education and so on. Certain common features may be listed without suggesting that they provide much uniformity. They are as follows:

1. There is everywhere the same diversity of structure, from large farms worked by wage labour and comparable to factories; through medium-sized farms with a stable workforce, family members or people contracted to the farm, plus seasonal labour; and traditional smallholdings worked at the personal level. Their takings range from high profits to meagre subsistence.

2. In contrast with the industrial society, employed persons on the land are probably outnumbered by the self-employed; and the latter may be landowners, secure tenants, tenants-at-will, family members, sharecroppers, or, as is customary in Africa, persons with a stake in the land through membership of organised village and tribal community life.

3. In general, agricultural wages and self-employed incomes are lower than in industry, with a wide disparity between workers on large estates and those on smaller farms. Smallholdings and tribal lands may support subsistence farming and they may also raise crops and cattle for the market.

4. Everywhere there is a drift from the land leaving the rural communities with a preponderance of older people, widows and those prone to ill health and invalidity.

Given such circumstances, the extension of a conventional programme of social security to the rural areas is by no means an easy task, nor is it necessarily a sufficient answer to the social security protection of persons in those areas. It meets the situation in areas where rural-urban communications are close enough for town and country to form one wage-paid community. Elsewhere, and particularly in developing countries, it has seldom proved possible to extend full cover to the countryside because of poor communications, the difficulties mentioned above, the question of identification and the problem of covering self-employed persons.

Agriculture provides a special challenge to social security policy makers and planners. It may well be that the proper answer will be found not in simply extending to the countryside the so-called traditional schemes and methods, or even adapting them, but in developing new forms of economic support other than individual cash benefits. Such forms of support might be crop insurance, natural disaster insurance, assisted marketing and new or better health services. However, a discussion of such matters would take us outside the scope of this book.

SOME BROADER ASPECTS OF BENEFIT 3

THE GENERAL STRUCTURE

So far, the development of social security and the dimensions within which it operates have been briefly described. It is now time to look at the end-product — what social security provides to individuals and families. In this chapter and immediately succeeding chapters, attention is focused on the material benefits, the essential purpose of the whole concept, and on the various conditions which are attached to the claiming and receipt of those benefits.

A former Director-General of the ILO, Wilfred Jenks, addressing the New Zealand Institute of International Affairs at Wellington in 1971, said as follows:

Nothing in the history of social policy has transformed the life of the common man more radically than the assurance that, in the event of loss of income through accident, poor health, unemployment, death of the breadwinner or any other misfortune, he will not be forced into destitution.[1]

On the way towards this transformation, social insurance was thought of as the first essential pillar of security — a pillar of income replacement during the period when earnings were interrupted or had stopped provision of medical care for insured persons and, often, their families.

The concept has been progressively extended. A third pillar has been constructed, supporting by a variety of programmes of financial assistance those whose means and resources are meagre or whose family responsibilities or exceptional needs make a special claim on the community. And still the structure has grown, so that social security may well now encourage and encompass developments such as special tax allowances, subsidised housing and food, and even the provision of transport.

Advanced programmes of social security can no longer be thought of as just income replacement systems. In many industrialised countries schemes have become complex and comprehensive vehicles for what are called "social transfers", the means of redistributing cash, goods and services to the needier sections of the community. At the same time, however, it is recognised that aspirations go beyond mere subsistence to a guaranteed basic standard of living. The requirements of individuals in these societies and their understanding of their security needs, with the emphasis on general well-being within the total environment of life and work, obviously differ from the needs of those in developing countries. The form of protection which has evolved in industrialised communities, even if thought to be justified, is a distant prospect in countries still in the process of development.

The ILO has recognised that, in planning initial schemes of cash benefit, realistic standards have to be set, and has concentrated attention on framing levels of benefit provision which can be flexibly introduced and applied by different countries at suitable stages in their national development process.

In the exploration of the benefits which social security schemes provide, it is most convenient to take the Social Security (Minimum Standards) Convention, 1952 (No. 102), as a starting point. And while this approach primarily concerns benefits which give protection after the event, it is salutary to bear in mind that effective social security owes as much to preventive measures as to compensation and cure.

The benefits which are described in Convention No. 102 are commonly grouped into branches for organisational and functional purposes. The benefits are: medical care, sickness and maternity benefits; unemployment benefit; family benefits; employment injury benefits; and invalidity, old-age and survivors' benefits.

Although these benefits seek to protect covered persons from a whole range of different hazards, they have a number of elements in common. With the exception of unemployment benefit, they have some biological association — they relate to disease, injury, childbirth, old age, death and the addition of a child or of children to the family. Secondly, they can all put the worker's income from his job under pressure, and may result in its being reduced, interrupted or lost. Thirdly, they can conveniently be placed into certain broad categories of hazard or risk. The contingencies of curable sickness, maternity and unemployment are usually of a short-term duration and should cause, at worst, temporary loss of earnings, whereas invalidity, old age and the events following the death of a breadwinner have longer-term implications; prolonged structural unemployment presents its own problem. The inherent risks of the work-bench and the factory give us another natural classification in employment injury benefits.

Loss of wages is not the only financial hazard. Any illness may involve expenditure on treatment. Serious illness or disablement can involve considerable expense on the prolonged and specialised treatment which may be required to minimise the loss or impairment of the normal functions of life. A further group of contingencies embraces the continuing and the emergency expenses of family dependants, and funeral expenses, whether anticipated or unlooked for.

THE PROGRESSIVE DEVELOPMENT OF BENEFIT GROUPS

While sophisticated and complex systems of social security are found in many industrialised countries, none started with anything like a programme fully covering all contingencies. Social security is introduced by stages, an uncontroversial start often being made in the area of employment injury benefits protection.

Thereafter, the pace and type of extension of protection depend on the priorities which are perceived in the different countries. Some have taken the view that medical care, sickness and maternity benefits have a more immediate impact, with their short qualifying periods which bring quick results and establish confidence in the system — particularly important where many of the workers are young and concerned more with current than future problems. On the other hand, priority may be given to the plight of the elderly, and the importance of laying foundations for the future — schemes which will ultimately come to fruition in benefits sufficient to support the older members of society or persons forced prematurely to retire from regular work through illness. An advantage of starting with the long-term benefit branch, with the use of the social insurance technique, is that in the early years of such a programme funds are accumulated which, if carefully invested, can promote national development.

Perhaps the order in which benefits are introduced is not of the greatest consequence. What is vital is that the social security programme should be seen and planned as a developed whole from the outset. The most pressing needs of the country and the ability of the institutions involved to cope with the programme and to organise and administer it efficiently should be taken into consideration.

SOCIAL INSURANCE AND SOCIAL ASSISTANCE

The techniques of providing benefit through social insurance were developed, in the first instance, for employed persons. The administrative difficulties which stand in the way of covering self-employed persons have been touched upon in the previous chapter. While, in principle, unemployment benefit and employment injury benefits are not available to the self-employed, voluntary insurance for long-term pension benefits is often arranged if compulsory coverage is not found possible.

In contrast, social assistance measures are usually all-embracing. Basically the right to benefit flows from membership of the community and the community finds the funds — more will be said of this in Chapter 12 on the financing of social security. The strict differentiation between schemes of social assistance and social insurance generally remains, although the distinction is beginning to lose its focus in many industrialised countries. Indeed, when a country has achieved virtually universal coverage, urban and rural, with an income-related contributory benefit scheme, the source of funds has been spread uniformly over the whole community and has become in effect a general income tax. In such a situation, there would be no need to impose detailed contribution conditions on the award of contributory benefit; status as a covered person, plus a residence condition, would be a sufficient qualification, very close to that for assistance. Assistance rules would still be required to cope with, for example, a recent arrival from abroad, a deserted wife without contributory status, or a beneficiary whose means were still insufficient to cover essential needs. However, this paragraph anticipates a more general look at qualifying conditions.

QUALIFYING CONDITIONS

In every scheme there are certain conditions to be met before benefits can be awarded. It goes without saying, perhaps, that the first condition requires proof of the contingency for which the scheme or branch of benefit was designed. For example, when employment injury benefit provisions are invoked, evidence must be produced of an accident at work (or occupational disease); claimants for old-age benefit must satisfy the authorities that they have reached the age stipulated in the legislation; and so on.

Secondly, it is necessary to know that the claimant is properly within the coverage of the scheme or branch of benefit.

Finally, as in most cases awards are dependent upon the actual reduction or cessation of earnings or upon the need to incur certain expenses, it is necessary to be satisfied that the various conditions in these respects are fulfilled. If the prescribed rules require, for instance, that a person be insured at a particular point of time and these rules are not satisfied, there is no point in testing the other conditions. Even when such a rule is satisfied, insurance schemes often stipulate that a minimum period, varying in length with the type of benefit, must be served by the person concerned before title can be conceded. Such a test is necessary in insurance-based schemes to reduce the possibility that persons will seek to enter covered employment knowing or fearing that an event which gives rise to benefit title has occurred or is imminent. This particular problem is of little or no significance in countries which have moved to universal or near universal coverage since "bad risks" will already have been allowed for in the financial structure.

Under benefit schemes which are publicly financed or of a social assistance nature, the conditions relating to status are somewhat different. Since the applicant is not personally insured under the scheme and therefore cannot be identified from insurance records, some other method of determining eligibility for benefits must be introduced. A simple test of nationality or, in the case of non-nationals or persons born abroad, of regular residence of the country under whose law the claim is being made, is often all that is required; for the longer-term benefits such as invalidity or old-age benefit, the conditions may be more demanding and may require continuous residence in the country for a minimum number of years.

When proof of the contingency has been supplied, and the other qualifying conditions have been met, the form and amount of the appropriate benefit can be established and payment can be made or services provided. Medical care involves an element of discretion, for the medical authorities will decide what kind of treatment is to be given, where and how it is to be made available, and for how long. Even so, the rules will often set maximum limits which may only be exceeded in exceptional cases — limits of cost, or of duration of the benefit.

The criteria for benefits in respect of families stands rather apart from the other branches of benefit listed in Convention No. 102, and will be discussed in Chapter 11.

THE LEVEL OF BENEFITS

Social progress is an expensive process and it is the variety of benefits provided and the level of such benefits which make it so. How much social security can a country afford when balancing the various social and economic considerations involved? This is a world-wide problem which takes different forms in countries at different stages of economic and social development or with different economic structures and traditions. Nevertheless, the problem is of concern everywhere, and has sharpened in recent years with fluctuations in the level of economic growth. It is discussed in some detail in Chapter 13.

It was recognised quite early that, given the widely differing pattern of needs and resources available, benefit levels must be geared in a realistic fashion to the various social and economic constraints which apply in different countries. The ILO Conventions take these factors into account and put forward flexible standards for the levels of benefit.

In this part of the chapter, the levels of cash benefits provided under schemes of social security, as distinct from levels of medical service, are discussed. Of the latter, all that needs to be said at this point is that, when benefits are provided by way of services, it is the quality as well as the range of services which demands attention. Quality, an essential criterion of the provision of service, is notoriously difficult to measure and nowhere more so than in the case of medical care where the benefits are provided wholly or mainly in terms of service. The issues involved will be discussed in Chapter 4.

Changes have occurred over the years in the general levels of cash benefits; these changes reflect the social and economic thinking of the times, and also the political possibilities, since they have to be implemented by legislative processes.

Though there are early instances of relating benefit rates to wages earned, on the whole this method came late to the social security scene. More often than not, benefit rates were pitched at a level thought to be adequate for subsistence needs. More recent ideas included the establishment of scales of payment which would enable people to maintain, while on benefit, a standard of living reasonably comparable to that which they had enjoyed while in work. Of course, this did not provide 100 per cent replacement of wages, but a proportion of them, and it certainly made "social security" more meaningful for salaried employees and workers on high wages.

Different levels of benefit are often found in respect of the same contingency. A low rate of benefit for short-term sickness may, for example, be justified by some on the grounds that a person can, or should be able to, manage satisfactorily in the first few days of sickness. On the other hand, it can be argued that a claimant cannot suddenly cut back on usual expenditure, and so a high rate of benefit, close to normal income level, should be given.

A lower level of benefit for old-age pensions is frequently found. The justification put forward for this is that needs in old age are fewer and that lifestyles change in retirement. The contrary view is that the pension is the sole source of income for most people, probably for many years. It is reasoned that a higher rather than a lower income is needed since the pensioner becomes increasingly dependent on others as the years advance.

Comparatively high rates of employment injury benefits are often found. The reason for this may well be historical rather than logical, as will be seen in Chapter 6.

In the midst of these various, and sometimes contradictory, arguments it would be very surprising if the differences in attitudes, traditions and financial practices from one country to another, or even within the country itself, did not lead to divergencies in levels of benefit, and this is in fact what a study of the various ranges and levels of benefit reveals.

Convention No. 102 recognises two approaches to fixing levels of benefit, and gives both equal weight. Basically these can be described as, on the one hand, levels based on a proportion of wages (earnings-related) and, on the other, levels based on the cost of subsistence. The drafters of the Convention went to some length to establish fair and reasonable rules for ascertaining and comparing the economic significance of benefit levels in different countries. The Convention seeks to establish appropriate levels of benefit for a country by using a "typical wage" for the country concerned and measuring the adequacy of the level of benefit by reference to that wage. The purchasing power of wages might be said to be roughly proportional to a country's effective wealth and benefit levels cannot, in any case, be higher than earnings from work. So the Convention is concerned with setting standards in line with a country's ability to reach those standards, rather than with fixing some theoretical benefit level to be applied internationally.

Where a scheme is intended to provide flat-rate subsistence levels of benefit, the Convention specifies that reference should be made to the wage of a typical unskilled male worker, while if the benefit is earnings-related, the range must embrace persons who earn up to the level of a skilled manual worker's wage. The reason for the latter requirement is that national schemes usually fix a maximum for earnings-related benefit; and the maximum should not be so low that it defeats the object, which is to provide appropriate benefits over a reasonably wide spectrum of earnings. Minimum benefit, if it is defined at all in legislation, often falls well below the subsistence level.

Another interesting aspect of this Convention is that the definition of typical skilled and unskilled workers is based more on statistical analysis than on a prescribed description; the same methods are also used to define adequate levels of social security benefits in later, more advanced, Conventions such as the Employment Injury Benefits Convention, 1946 (No. 121), and the Invalidity, Old-Age and Survivors' Benefits Convention, 1967 (No. 128).

In practice, it will be found that there are limits to the types and levels of benefits provided. A benefit for lost earnings will rarely be less than one-quarter of a wage for an unskilled worker; there are numbers of countries in which the level reaches 100 per cent of an individual's wage. The distinction between earnings-related benefits and subsistence level benefits appears at first sight to be fundamental, but they are often partially applied together − for example, the benefit may consist of two elements, one varying with the person's wage, and the other varying with the number of dependants. Again, although minimum rates are only sometimes established, it is an almost universal practice to set maximum rates.

The explanation for the difference in benefit levels between one country and another, or between one scheme and another, lies in the economic, philosophical or ideological approach to the systems, their functions and aims. It is to be expected that, where the approach is to encourage personal rather than collective responsibility, the system will emphasise voluntary supplementation of basic protection. In such cases, the basic social security system will be geared to providing a minimum level of benefit, though in some instances there is mandatory association with a second tier system providing earnings-related cover, up to a certain earnings limit. Other countries have taken the view that social protection should be all-embracing and leave little or no room, or necessity, for augmentation by savings, private insurance or supplementary schemes.

Levels of benefits in family programmes are almost as diverse as the number of countries which have such programmes. So in Convention No. 102 a standard was fixed which took account of total benefits made available in kind, as well as any made available in cash — 3 per cent of an unskilled worker's wage for each protected child where the scheme has a limited coverage or 1.5 per cent for each child where the scheme extends to the whole population.

MAINTENANCE OF THE VALUE OF BENEFITS

Before turning to a detailed description of the individual benefits, and closing this chapter on the general aspects of benefits, a comment should be made on the need not only to set initial levels and rates of benefit correctly but also to maintain these levels once the benefits are in payment. In a period of rapid inflation such as that which the world has undergone in recent years, the erosion of the purchasing power of social security benefits can have dramatic and unfortunate consequences. A social security scheme which does not adapt its benefits to changes in the value of money is not fulfilling its original purpose. Many authorities have responded to this problem and have periodically carried out general revaluations of the benefits in payment only to find, a year or so later, that the new scales have again become inadequate.

Hence a growing number of social security schemes now incorporate legislative provisions for the automatic adjustment of their benefits in line with the general level of prices or wages. The International Labour Conference, in its Income Security Recommendation, 1944 (No. 67), foresaw this problem. The later Conventions in 1952, in 1964 and in 1967 all confirm the principle put forward in 1944, namely that rates of benefit ought to be reviewed following any substantial change in the general level of earnings or in the cost of living.

In the case of short-term benefits, where the average claim does not last very long and where the level of benefit reflects the level of the claimant's recent wages, no great difficulty arises unless inflation is catastrophically rapid. It is with the long-term pension benefits that the major problem is found. Here the claimant may suffer a double blow if nothing is done to adjust the pension in line with current levels of earnings or living costs. Frequently the level of the pension itself is calculated on past earnings over the employment life of the claimant. Unless these past earnings are reassessed to give them an adequate current value, the rate of pension may be unduly low in relation to wages or to the cost of living at the time it is awarded. Once in payment, unless some adjustment is undertaken from time to time, the value of the pension will depreciate more and more during periods of inflation.

Note

[1] Wilfred Jenks: *Social security as a world problem*, Occasional Papers in Industrial Relations, No. 6 (Victoria University of Wellington. Industrial Relations Centre in conjunction with the New Zealand Institute of International Affairs, 1972).

MEDICAL CARE 4

MEDICAL CARE BENEFIT

All the risks for which conventional social security is designed are related to health. They are directly related in the case of employment injury, sickness, invalidity, disablement and maternity; and indirectly related in the case of old-age and survivors' pensions, family benefit and unemployment benefit, since these benefits are intended to maintain the beneficiaries in a state of adequate nutrition and good health. The connection between ill-health and poverty, with each being a principal cause of the other, does not need to be emphasised. So it is not surprising to find that medical care is the first of the social security benefits listed in the Social Security (Minimum Standards) Convention, 1952 (No. 102), and it is not unreasonable to look at medical care benefit against the background of overall health protection.

Convention No. 102 establishes that medical care benefit is provided to maintain, restore or improve the health of the persons protected and their ability to work and to attend to their personal needs. The minimum content of the benefit covers general practitioner care, including home visits; specialist care in hospitals and similar institutions for in-patients and out-patients, and such specialist care as may be available outside hospitals; essential pharmaceutical supplies; pre-natal, confinement and post-natal care by medical practitioners or qualified midwives; and hospitalisation where necessary. To this the Medical Care and Sickness Benefits Convention, 1969 (No. 130), adds dental care and medical rehabilitation including necessary appliances.

Administratively, it is easier to pay a cash benefit than to ensure that the facilities and health personnel required to provide medical care are available when they are needed by a sick or injured person. It is essential to make as sure of this as possible. But it cannot be assumed, in starting or expanding a social security medical care system, that the protected persons and the health personnel will behave exactly as they have done before. Demands for care will rise to meet further perceived needs and expenditure will increase. Although it used to be assumed that the introduction of a comprehensive state medical service would improve health standards and that, consequently, the calls on medical care facilities should not increase and might in fact decline, nowhere has this happened.

It is fair to ask whether medical care must be provided with little or no charge and whether it must all be instantly available on demand. These are really questions about the allocation of limited resources to the maximum possible benefit of all, and how they are answered depends upon a variety of factors, such as the difference between industrialised countries, with one doctor for around 600 patients, and developing countries, where the ratio can exceed 1 to 20,000. The fact remains that any enacted programme must work and the programme must promise no more than can be delivered.

MEDICAL CARE SYSTEMS

The organisation of social security medical care naturally differs according to the characteristics of the country concerned. Political considerations will dictate one pattern where private enterprise and local autonomy are favoured and another where there is a planned economy and centralised government control. Historical factors play their part as do the size of the country and the spread of population. Even so, two broad systems of organisation have developed — the indirect and the direct.

The indirect system is usually found in industrialised countries. In such countries, a large establishment of health professionals in private practice and of hospital and other facilities already existed when social insurance schemes providing medical care were first launched. It was found practical for the social security institution to enter into a variety of contracts to secure medical care for insured persons, usually on the basis that a fee would be paid for each medical service provided. This fee-for-service method is unlikely to be simple. Prices must be agreed for a long list of medical items and prescriptions. There are complex administrative arrangements for the presentation and payment of accounts, and obvious problems of verification and control of the services provided. Some part of this may be avoided by paying fixed sums towards defined courses of treatment, leaving it to the beneficiary to meet the difference between that fixed sum and the actual cost of the treatment. However, such demands on the beneficiary can be considerable.

In another variant of the fee-for-service method, the patient pays the medical bill and is then reimbursed, in whole or in part, by the social security institution. Finally, under the indirect system, a few countries use the capitation method for paying general practitioners — a fixed amount of money is paid for a fixed period during which doctors undertake responsibility for the medical care of the people registered with them.

Under the direct system, the social security institution itself owns, operates and controls the necessary medical facilities. The responsibility of the institution thus extends to the quality and efficiency of the services as well as their financial cost. An administrative framework, designed to make the most efficient use of its resources, must be created and the medical facilities required must be set up. In the initial stages, capital expenditure may be particularly high. Personnel are usually paid by salary, which is determined according to personal factors, professional qualifications and levels of responsibility. The whole staff works as a team and patients are transferred to the appropriate specialist or hospital as the case may require.

It is argued in favour of the direct system that, provided the medical services are organised by competent people and efficiently administered, operational costs and the physical demands on supplies and services can be contained within reasonable limits; that an adequate geographical distribution of medical facilities and personnel can be achieved; and also that better co-ordination with other agencies, including the public health services, is possible. It may be criticised, however, for a tendency to bureaucracy and over-centralisation, and for the virtual denial to the patient of a choice of physician, with the consequential loss of the important personal relationship between patient and doctor.

QUALIFYING CONDITIONS AND DURATION OF BENEFIT

In a number of social security systems, persons who require medical care must satisfy a qualifying period of employment or contributions in order to demonstrate that they are in the category of people for whom the benefit is intended. Convention No. 102 authorises "such qualifying period as may be considered necessary to preclude abuse". In practice, the detailed conditions vary from so many hours or weeks of employment in, say, the last three months, to something like six contribution months during the past year. Some countries match the qualifying conditions to those for sickness benefit, arguing that it is illogical to provide the money and not the care or the care without the money. In general, however, qualifying conditions are kept to a minimum, since the aim is to make medical care easily accessible.

There is, of course, no question of a qualifying period for medical care following employment injury, and the Medical Care and Sickness Benefits Recommendation, 1969 (No. 134), suggests that qualifying periods should be abolished generally.

Most systems set a limit on the duration, or the total cost, of the treatment of a medical episode, although the tendency is to be more liberal or to abolish limits altogether. Convention No. 102 lays down a limit of 26 weeks, but allows for continuation thereafter while sickness benefit is being paid or for diseases accepted as needing prolonged care. The Medical Care and Sickness Benefits Convention, 1969 (No. 130), sanctions the removal of limits.

The schemes of some countries continue to provide medical benefit for a period of, say, six months after a person's coverage under the social security programme has otherwise ceased. And some countries provide medical care, without limit of time, for specified groups such as the elderly. The latter is a most valuable benefit, since it is with increasing age that medical problems multiply and personal resources diminish.

HOSPITALISATION

Some countries started their programme of social security medical care by providing only for treatment in hospitals, excluding all other care such as that given by doctors in their surgeries or on house calls; and some, with limited resources, continue with this narrower provision. The case for it is that hospitalisation is the really expensive risk faced by covered persons — the so-called "catastrophic risk". The consequence is that the pattern of care is distorted because people try to get all their care in hospital, even though this is the most expensive way for the country to provide it. So more hospitals than are necessary are built and, once the programme has been extended to cover treatment by visiting doctors, too much of the available money is found to have been devoted to surplus hospital beds. As will be explained later in this chapter, the need in developing countries is for primary medical care — concentration of scarce money and resources on expensive hospitals is the wrong priority.

COST SHARING

The term "cost sharing" refers to charges made at the point of delivery of medical care. It may mean a direct payment by the patient towards the cost of the service, such as a charge for a drug prescription; or, as has already been mentioned, it may mean that the patient has to pay the difference between a prescribed scale and what the doctor or hospital actually charges, or to pay a fixed percentage of that charge.

Cost sharing tends to be a controversial subject. A point of principle may be advanced — the purpose of social security is that the community can be relied upon to pay for the sick and that the social security contributions themselves (or, as the case may be, the scales of tax) constitute the cost-sharing mechanism; to require additional payments during sickness is contrary to the purpose of social security and could tempt insured persons to neglect their own health and that of any covered dependants. Against this it may be argued that, although medical care should be a basic human right, not all of it need invariably be delivered free of charge; on the contrary, it would be no bad thing to make people aware, by cost sharing, of the value of the medical benefits they are receiving.

Certainly, many countries continue to operate substantial cost-sharing arrangements. It is by no means unusual to find that a patient has to pay, for example, something between 25 and 40 per cent of the doctor's fees. Convention No. 102 recognises the practice, requiring only that cost sharing should be so designed as to avoid hardship. Few, if any, schemes fail to have a list of exemptions, such as old-age pensioners, persons in receipt of social assistance and other specified social security beneficiaries.

Substantial cost sharing can have side-effects. It may stand in the way of necessary treatment, leading subsequently to much higher expenditure than would have been necessary if the condition had been detected at an early stage. A patient who has to pay a fee to the doctor may be more likely to expect something tangible in return, such as one or more prescriptions for medicine, and the doctor may feel obliged to fulfil that expectation. If a unit charge per prescription is made by the doctor, or at the pharmacy or dispensary, there may be pressure from the patient, doctor or both to over-prescribe on any one occasion and some of the prescribed drugs may be wasted. And if cost sharing is selectively applied, say, to primary care by family doctors and not to hospitalisation, the pattern of supply can be expensively distorted by undue use of the free or less costly alternative.

The argument remains that cost sharing can come to the aid of the medical care budget, both directly in cash and indirectly by reducing utilisation. But it should be borne in mind that at least one-half of the total expenditure goes on not much more than 5 per cent of the population — those who are most seriously ill and who are therefore the most likely candidates for exemption from charges.

THE SITUATION IN DEVELOPING COUNTRIES

Much of what has been said so far relates to well-developed programmes of social security medical care. The situation in developing countries can be very different. Many have a markedly uneven spread of population as between rural areas and crowded urban centres. Population growth is high or even, in some regions, explosive. Mortality, particularly infant mortality, is high, and infectious diseases can still be described as rampant in many places, largely because of inadequate health services. In many developing countries, nearly one-half of the population is under the age of 15.

Against such a background, there are some developing countries with over 20,000 inhabitants to each doctor and over 2,000 inhabitants to each hospital bed — about ten times more than the corresponding ratios in industrialised countries. And the medical care services which do exist are very unequally distributed, as they are concentrated in larger urban centres to an even greater degree than the population itself. Furthermore, the facilities of the medical care services are usually overburdened and may involve the patient in heavy expense; pharmaceutical products are often especially costly. One of the most common findings in surveys of expenditure in developing countries is that the better-off members of the community, and a large proportion of the poorer people, spend a significant part of their family income on drugs.

The provision of medical care by employers is of some help. Occasionally this is voluntary, but some countries have labour laws which require specified enterprises to provide medical care for the workers and their families. Such laws are difficult to enforce and the medical care actually provided may be very limited. In many developing countries it is only in the public and parastatal sector that reasonably good medical care is available to employees and their dependants.

The role of social security

A number of developing countries, therefore, are turning to social security schemes for more general provision of medical care. Employment injury schemes meet the cost of medical care in the case of accidents at work and occupational diseases, while maternity insurance may cover the confinement expenses of employed women. In addition, there is the care provided free of charge (though to an extent varying with the country) at medical centres set up by the social security institutions operating within the framework of health and welfare services.

In common with other sections of social security, medical care schemes in developing countries tend to be introduced first for a limited group of employed persons and the extension of coverage is planned as a later development. This initial limitation of cover raises the problem of fairness. But the case for even a limited programme of medical care under social security is strong. In the report of a World Health Organisation study group in 1978,[1] the ILO has summarised the argument in the following terms:

(1)   It creates new and continuing allocations of resources that would not otherwise be available through public health budgets, whose share of general revenues has to be competed for among the demands from other government spending departments, probably on an annual and thus uncertain basis.

(2)   It stimulates and promotes the building up of hospitals, clinics, dispensaries and related facilities, which are not only valuable as treatment centres but also offer health professionals and auxiliaries new and increasing opportunities for employment which is both socially useful and remunerative.

(3) It thus supports increases in the number and skills of the available health manpower; indeed, emigration of doctors, which is of special concern in some developing countries, may well be curbed.

(4) It erodes the commercial private health sector, and relieves the public health services of care for the persons covered by social security, so assisting these services to concentrate their attention more effectively on care in areas that are especially badly served and for sections of the community as yet excluded from social security protection, and on improved preventive activities, for which such services are irreplaceable.

(5) It improves the health of the labour force so protected, thus increasing the productivity needed for economic development − and, more generally, contributes to raising living standards. In the words of the 1970 Joint ILO/WHO Committee, "each skilled worker represents a social investment (in his training, experience, etc.); therefore the maintenance of his health serves the good of the entire society".

(6) It has general support irrespective of political doctrine, and creates health awareness.

To the terms of the above report one should add, of course, that any system of social security medical care should be developed in close co-ordination with the overall national health plan and with the Health Ministry, especially as regards capital expenditure. Duplication, overlapping and competition for scarce resources must be avoided.

PRIMARY HEALTH CARE

There is world-wide recognition that the overriding need in developing countries is for primary health care. This concept was defined in the report [2] of an international conference, held in 1978 at Alma-Ata, USSR, in the following terms:

Primary health care addresses the main health problems in the community, providing promotive, preventive, curative and rehabilitative services. Since these services reflect and evolve from the economic conditions and social values of the country and its communities, they will vary by country and community, but will include at least: promotion of proper nutrition and an adequate supply of safe water; basic sanitation; maternal and child care, including family planning; immunisation against the major infectious diseases; prevention and control of locally endemic diseases; education concerning prevailing health problems and the methods of preventing and controlling them; and appropriate treatment for common diseases and injuries.

The object of primary health care organisation is to make the maximum use of available resources of personnel and equipment by employing them to the best advantage at each level from village health posts through district clinics and health centres to central hospitals. A mix of educational, preventive and curative service should be provided at each level. At the base there should be a large body of trained community health workers, and each successive tier should have its appropriate complement of general and specialist nursing staff, midwives and ancillary health workers, medical practitioners and hospital services. The system should make the fullest use of low-cost technology, for example, by relying on the model list of about 200 essential drugs recommended by World Health Organisation experts.[3]

The role of social security

Primary health care clearly cannot be achieved through the activities of the hard-pressed health sector alone, even though that sector has the key responsibility for strategy. All the sectors concerned with economic affairs, including social security, may be enlisted to play a part. Co-ordination between agencies providing medical care is essential in such matters as the following:

- sharing the available human and material resources of staff, premises and equipment;
- the joint planning of financial resources intended for capital investment in the construction of health facilities;
- collaboration as appropriate on the management of current expenditure, for example, in training, publicity and transport;
- team work amongst health personnel employed by different agencies;
- the joint development of national education and training programmes, involving the use of all suitable medical facilities; and
- the application of uniform and comparable methods of collecting health, and related, statistics.

THE RISING COST OF MEDICAL CARE UNDER SOCIAL SECURITY

Cost, and the question of how it might be controlled, must always be a matter of concern to governments and to organisations of workers and employers. In recent years expenditure on medical care has been rapidly increasing, both absolutely and in relation to other comparable costs. Indeed, the rate of increase often outpaces the rate of cost increase for cash benefits.

Although the problem of rising costs is so far being felt most severely in a number of industrialised countries with well-developed medical care systems which offer extensive population coverage under a social security scheme, it must be expected to emerge in developing countries as they introduce or expand such programmes. Thus, for developing countries too, the problem, though perhaps not immediate, is a real one.

The main causes are not hard to find, although it is difficult to put a figure on any one cause, or to say how far the increased cost is the result of greater use of services or higher prices paid for them. The causes include better public awareness of, and general concern for, medical care; the availability of new and costly forms of treatment; and increasing expenditure on drugs. There are also the demands of expanding populations, coupled with the continuing increase in the proportion of elderly people. Hospital costs reflect higher wage and salary levels. In the 1960s it was forecast that some countries would be devoting more than 10 per cent of their gross national product to health services by the end of the century. The forecast is likely to be realised sooner than that.

A detailed study by the ILO of the rising cost of medical care under social security was followed by a meeting of experts in Geneva in 1977. While recognising that measures to curb the growth of medical care expenditure were of limited effect when confronted by the changing age structure of the population and medical progress, the experts emphasised the importance of primary health care as opposed to sophisticated and expensive hospital treatment. They called for an optimum distribution of all the available resources. They considered that preventive measures should play an increasingly important part in social security programmes. And they recommended that the responsible authorities should be given more powers to control and monitor the operation of such programmes.

Various cost control measures which are used in a number of countries have already been discussed in this chapter. These include: cost sharing; limits on the duration of, and reimbursement for, treatment; and limits on the provision of drugs.

Because of the high cost of hospitalisation, administrative effort may profitably be directed towards reducing the average length of stay in hospital or towards scrutinising the need for in-patient treatment at all in particular cases. Much needed and costly hospital bed-space may be released through the provision of convalescent facilities. Action in this area calls for the careful recording and analysis of statistics of hospital use and, in particular, of the use of specialised equipment and highly trained technical, medical and surgical personnel. Such equipment and personnel will not realise their full potential and value unless they are located in such a way that they are regularly and systematically employed. Good communication between hospitals, clinics and health posts is also important in this context, as speedy, effective treatment results in a saving of cost to the system.

Notes

[1] WHO: *Financing of health services*, WHO Technical Report Series, No. 625, Annex 6 (Geneva, 1978).

[2] idem: *Primary health care*, Report of the International Conference, Alma-Ata, USSR, 6-12 September 1978 (Geneva, 1978).

[3] idem: *The selection of essential drugs*, WHO Technical Report Series, No. 615 (Geneva, 1977).

SICKNESS AND MATERNITY BENEFIT. FUNERAL BENEFIT 5

SHORT-TERM BENEFITS

Although the contingencies are distinct — sickness is a morbid condition and a normal uncomplicated pregnancy is not — the similarities between sickness benefit and maternity benefit are close enough for them frequently to be linked together administratively in a single short-term benefit scheme. Normally, they involve interruption of employment for a relatively short period, and normally they attract the same level of benefit during that period. Occasionally, the morbid condition may be prolonged into long-term invalidity; and some maternity schemes extend modified cover to non-wage-earning mothers.

As will be seen in Chapter 12, the financial system underlying the provision of sickness and maternity cash benefits is the same, and it is relatively straightforward in comparison with the financing of pensions. Indeed, in a society in which a few hundred persons can be grouped together and in which medical services are available, a sickness and maternity insurance scheme can be evolved and run successfully with little difficulty. And, although the contingency is even more distinct, such a scheme can also pay a funeral benefit on the death of a covered person, or a dependant, without administrative or financial difficulty. The two other short-term benefits are for unemployment (see Chapter 10) and for initial incapacity as a result of an employment injury (see Chapter 6).

A typical scheme also provides medical care and maternity services, with personnel and facilities provided either directly by the scheme itself, or indirectly through contract arrangements with private medical practitioners and private or public hospitals. In a different form of government organisation, found in the countries of Eastern Europe or in the United Kingdom and in New Zealand, for example, the payment of cash benefit is the responsibility of the social security administration while, quite separately, medical care and maternity services are provided by the public health authority.

SICKNESS BENEFIT

Sickness benefit is payable when an insured person has to stop work because of some medical condition. Such a stoppage usually entails the reduction or suspension of earnings, and the cash benefit is designed to replace, in whole or in part, the earnings so lost.

The awarding or adjudicating authority must, of course, be satisfied as to the claimant's medical condition. For this reason, it is usual to require a certificate from a qualified medical practitioner indicating both the nature of the condition and the fact that it necessitates absence from work. In places where qualified medical practitioners are not available, or the medical services are working under pressure, practical rules have to be devised for the acceptance of other evidence, including even limited self-certification by the claimant as to his or her own condition.

The question of incapacity for work is crucial. Circumstantial evidence is as important as the medical opinion. For example, a condition which might be incapacitating to a miner may not prevent a clerk from working. Also, the incapacity is essentially temporary; the illness will clear up under treatment and the claimant will then go back to work. On the other hand, it may be apparent from the outset that the person concerned will be unable to resume work in the future. In that case an awkward question will have to be asked — will the claimant recover sufficiently to be no longer "incapable of work", even though he or she is unable to return to the job previously held? The question is hypothetical but it illustrates how the administration of sickness benefit has its own peculiar problems. Where that hypothetical question does not arise, and the medical condition is such that the beneficiary is obviously going to remain incapable of work, many schemes will continue to pay sickness benefit until the claimant's rights have been exhausted and will then replace it by long-term invalidity benefit or assistance. More is said below about the duration of entitlement to sickness benefit.

Most schemes pay sickness benefit only when incapacity persists beyond, say, three working days, a waiting period that is sanctioned by the Social Security (Minimum Standards) Convention, 1952 (No. 102). The principal reason for imposing the waiting period is to save expense, because brief illnesses account for a larger percentage of the total, and the cost of processing these cases is disproportionately high. It can be reasonably argued that no appreciable hardship is caused to a person who occasionally goes without wages for a few days, but one who suffers a number of short spells of incapacity in quick succession may be unfairly penalised by the waiting days rule. More developed schemes will often waive waiting days at the beginning of the second or subsequent spell of illness when it follows soon after the previous spell.

There is also a trend towards involving employers more closely in the actual payment of sickness benefit for the first so many days of incapacity.

It is not unusual for employers to supplement benefit, up to full wages, for short spells of incapacity. If they also handle the benefit, this serves to reduce duplication of work and the movement of documents, with a consequent saving of expense. The employer's active involvement may also improve the control of these short-term claims.

The determination of the levels of benefit in any scheme is a matter for the responsible social security authorities. Convention No. 102 expects the following minimum standards:

(a) where the scheme provides a basic flat rate, this should be enough, when added to any family allowance available during the illness, to make 45 per cent of what a typical labourer, with a wife and two children, would have by way of wages plus family allowance while in work; or

(b) where the scheme provides wage-related benefit, this should be enough, when added to any family allowance available during the illness, to make 45 per cent of what the claimant himself had by way of wages and family allowances while in work — over a range of wages up to that of a skilled worker with a wife and two children.

These are modest requirements, representing a small rate of benefit for many wage earners. Convention No. 102 sets realistic and flexible levels to which even the least developed country may aspire. Most countries adopt a simple formula which effectively exceeds these minima — a more generous percentage of the previous wage, or a flat rate which is reviewed from time to time in the light of the cost of living or changes in an index of prices or wages. The benefit itself may include an element for wife and children or this may be dealt with in a separate system of family allowances.

The Medical Care and Sickness Benefits Convention, 1969 (No. 130), while not displacing the earlier Convention No. 102, sets a further target to be aimed at — 60 per cent instead of the 45 per cent mentioned so far.

The Maternity Protection Convention (Revised), 1952 (No. 103), requires a benefit level of two-thirds where cash benefits are based on previous earnings. Still, these are not absolute standards. Those who determine what rates to put in their legislation must seek an optimum level, balancing one consideration with another. They will consider the cost to the community and the question of social priorities; and they should provide a benefit which is adequate to remove anxiety about living expenses. When the contributory benefit scheme is accompanied by an assistance scheme, they will try to set the level of the former higher than the subsistence level of the latter, so that the contributor can see a return for the money contributed; but the benefit level should ideally not be so high as to be a disincentive to return to work.

As mentioned above, because of the waiting days rule, the isolated very short illness may not be covered, but those illnesses which last not many days longer are also time-consuming and expensive to administer. Nor is there sufficient time for the social security office to verify that the incapacity for work was genuine. For these reasons, some schemes impose more than three waiting days (perhaps making a payment later when incapacity is prolonged), or restrict the rate of benefit payable for short spells of incapacity. The longer-term and serious illness is, however, a different matter as further medical opinion can more easily be obtained, if thought necessary, and the progress of the claim can be monitored.

A lengthy illness can drain a beneficiary's own savings, and there may be a case for increasing the level of benefit after a month or so, to acknowledge the consequences of a long period without wages. Conversely, in insurance-based schemes, both the rate and the duration of benefit may fluctuate, according to the length of the claimant's contribution record. These considerations, and the apparent contradiction between what may be seen as social need and what may be seen as financial orthodoxy, again illustrate the kind of difficulty which may face those with responsibility for planning the scheme.

Sometimes the rate of sickness benefit is reduced while the patient is being maintained in hospital at the expense of the scheme, or otherwise at public cost. Family allowances are normally untouched but, as regards the amount of the basic benefit and the persons who are to receive it, a surprising diversity is found. For instance, in some countries, the patient in hospital may receive nothing, while one-half of the benefit is paid to any dependants. Elsewhere, the patient may be paid "pocket money" of up to one-half of the benefit, and the patient's dependants the remainder. Convention No. 102 lays down a precise and logical rule: any portion of the benefit in excess of the value of the maintenance of the patient must be paid to the patient's dependants.

In the context of social security, sickness is a temporary condition to be matched by a temporary benefit, available for a period during which the condition may be expected to clear up. For a condition which persists beyond that period, other arrangements have to be made.

Under the first German insurance scheme, the maximum duration of sickness benefit was only 13 weeks. Later, 26 weeks became standard practice in many countries. (In a few schemes, a less favourable formula prescribes "26 weeks in any period of 52 weeks".) This was a convenient interim solution because most illnesses which last as long as 26 weeks are probably likely to continue indefinitely. It is also the figure accepted in Convention No. 102.

As medicine became better able to promise recovery from diseases previously regarded as incurable, a more constructive view of the responsibility of social insurance began to be taken. Schemes have progressively been modified so as to permit payment of sickness benefit beyond 26 weeks when there is a likelihood of cure or improvement. The Medical Care and Sickness Benefits Convention, 1969 (No. 130), lays down a minimum of one year, but often the possibility of recovery from a persistent disease cannot be written off so soon. In most advanced countries, the limit for the duration of sickness benefit is now set at two or three years. And if, at the end of the day, a social security programme manages to pay invalidity pension at the same rate as sickness benefit, while medical care is provided through a state-wide public health service, the limitation has been abolished altogether.

MATERNITY BENEFIT

It is a measure of the international concern for the working mother, prompted no doubt by the growth in the number of women entering industrial and factory life, that one of the earliest Conventions to be adopted by the ILO at its first annual International Labour Conference was the Maternity Protection Convention, 1919 (No. 3). The purpose of Convention No. 3 was to ensure that a woman worker should be able to sustain and care for herself and her baby over the period immediately before and after her confinement.

Although Convention No. 3 was updated in some of its details in 1952, particularly in relation to the level of benefit provided, which should be not less than two-thirds of previous earnings when the system is one of earnings-related social insurance, the principles running through it remain as valid today as when it was adopted. It was laid down that there should be abstention from work for a period of at least 12 weeks, starting six weeks before the expected week of confinement but, in any event, continuing for six weeks after the actual confinement; that medical care should be provided by a doctor or certificated midwife; that cash payments should be available for maintenance during this time (financed in such a way that the cost did not fall exclusively on the employer); that the mother should be guaranteed reinstatement in her job (even if illness after the confinement prolonged the period of maternity leave); and, finally, that arrangements should be made to permit her to nurse the baby during working hours.

The labour legislation of many countries requires employers to grant paid maternity leave and to comply in other respects with the requirements of Convention No. 3. In the absence of adequate protection in this form, responsibility falls upon the social security institutions. Maternity benefits may be derived from any one of several sources. These include the classic health insurance system which provides cash sickness and maternity benefits (customarily at the same rates), together with medical care, and more comprehensive social insurance programmes which have a separate maternity benefit branch. Alternatively, measures which are directed towards providing support for the family generally may make special provision for pregnancy and childbirth, and for the working mother. Self-contained schemes devoted to maternity benefit alone may also be

41

found. Medical care arrangements, equally applicable to maternity benefit, have already been described in Chapter 4.

The 12-week or 13-week maternity benefit period has acquired such general acceptance that it has almost become a fixed tradition, but practice is tending towards longer periods, anything up to six months in all, of maternity leave and benefit. Occasionally, a period of less than 12 weeks — or 12 weeks only with no extension for unexpectedly late confinement — is found. Whatever the length of the maternity benefit period formally prescribed, it is usual to concede entitlement to sickness benefit if, at the end of that period, the mother has not fully recovered from the effects of the confinement.

FUNERAL BENEFIT

A single-payment lump-sum benefit to assist in meeting the cost of burial and associated expenses on the death of an insured person has long been a feature of sickness insurance schemes. Most comprehensive social security programmes now feature it as an element in the long-term benefit and employment injury branches of the programme. The demand for this kind of benefit dates from the industrial conditions of the nineteenth century, when workers sought to avoid saddling their next of kin with the cost of their burial, or the alternative humiliation of a pauper funeral.

Funeral benefit is sometimes made available, not only in respect of the covered person, but on the death of the spouse, or of another member of the immediate family. The grant is paid to the person who meets or intends to meet the cost of the funeral, or it may be paid into the estate of the deceased. The amount varies. Frequently, it is quite a moderate sum which may be sufficient to meet the expense of a decent but modest funeral only. Other schemes, however, are designed to meet the actual cost of the funeral to within certain limits, or calculate the grant on the basis of, say, two months' wages or a proportion of the annual value of the deceased person's pension.

EMPLOYMENT INJURY BENEFIT 6

THE PROBLEM AND THE PRINCIPLE

Earlier chapters have shown that employment injury benefit, although perhaps not the oldest, is certainly the most widely adopted branch of comprehensive social security. Over the years legislators have used a variety of terminology to describe the contingency. Earlier legal provisions often used the term "workmen's compensation", and referred to incapacity which could be temporary or permanent, total or partial, and to prescribed diseases. The more recent legislation adopts the term "employment injury", which is used in the Social Security (Minimum Standards) Convention, 1952 (No. 102), to comprehend the consequences of accidents at work and of occupational diseases; and usually differentiates between the immediate incapacity for work, the residual disablement which may be the longer-term result and, of course, the needs of survivors in fatal cases.

A brief historical review provides useful background to the current scene. In the early days of industrialisation, if anyone suffered injury at work or otherwise, his remedy lay in action against the person who had caused the injury. However, an employee injured at work could hope for effective redress only from his employer, and the obstacles in his way were virtually insurmountable in anything but the simplest one-to-one relationship between them. The complexity of the working environment, the actions or shortcomings of fellow employees, foremen or supervisors, the inherent dangers of machinery, the lack of any formal avenue of procedure other than the ordinary courts — everything, it seemed, conspired to put the injured worker at a disadvantage and leave him helpless, with only private charity and the blanket provisions of the Poor Law to fall back on.

Some principle had to be forged to characterise the accident at work in such a way that its consequences could attract just and equitable remedies. The principle was derived from the consideration that any person who carries on economic activities by using machinery and the labour of other persons creates an organisation which, by its very nature, may result in accidental injury to those persons; and that such a person should have a responsibility to provide compensation in prescribed contingencies, without any question being raised as to whether the injury was attributable to fault on the part of the employer, the employee, or any third party. In the context of that responsibility, the amount of monetary redress and the provision of medical care should be set at a reasonable level and charged to the employer. Thus, in a rough and ready way, with no fault imputed to either side, the immediate consequences of the accident would be shared, with the employee continuing to draw a substantial part of his wages.

How the principle comes to be expressed in a form of words is discussed a little later on. In a number of countries, the creation of this system of compensation did not, and still does not, deprive the injured worker of the inherent right to claim damages under the general law if the worker considered that the circumstances in which the injury occurred justified such an action; but equally, in yet other countries, the injured person has no such redress.

EMPLOYER'S LIABILITY; WORKMEN'S COMPENSATION

From the outset, workmen's compensation was a statutory liability placed upon employers. As with many other business expenses, an employer can always take out commercial insurance to cover this liability, and often the governing legislation requires the employer to do so for the more effective protection of the covered employees. Levels and amounts of compensation vary from country to country but a typical benefit structure is made up of five elements, somewhat as follows:

1. *Medical and hospital treatment.* There is a prescribed scale of costs, with a limit on the total amount. The limit may be exceeded if treatment is only available outside the country. In countries where medical care is available at public cost, this obligation may be waived, except for specialist treatment if it is necessary and not so available.

2. *Temporary incapacity.* Two-thirds of wages are payable while incapacity is total, and two-thirds of loss of earning capacity (measured by comparing earnings before and after the accident) for partial incapacity. The award for partial incapacity may be commuted for a lump sum.

3. *Permanent total incapacity.* A lump sum of five years' earnings is payable. This may be increased by one-quarter if the injured worker needs constant attendance.

4. *Permanent partial incapacity.* A percentage of the grant for total incapacity, based on a standard schedule of defined injuries, is payable. This basis of assessment is discussed in more detail below.

5.   *Fatal cases*. A lump sum of four years' earnings, within a minimum and maximum limit, less anything already paid for permanent incapacity, is payable.

Failing agreement between the parties concerned, and invariably in fatal cases, the award of compensation is reserved to the responsible minister or court. Compensation payable to children is usually administered by the court.

While workmen's compensation has proved to be an adequate and acceptable method of dealing with an intricate problem to which there is no absolute solution, it has long been held that there are two notable weaknesses in the established structure. One is that disputed claims go to litigation in the courts, a procedure which can delay settlements and introduce an undesirable element of acrimony between the injured worker and the employer. In some countries the situation is eased by substituting for the expensive formalities of the ordinary courts the administrative jurisdiction of a Workmen's Compensation Commissioner. Even so, and despite the employer's insurance policy, there is still a conflict of interest between the worker and the person or institution liable to meet the cost of the worker's claim.

The other weakness lies in the fact that, when the injury has resulted in serious permanent disablement or death, some, though certainly not all, workmen's compensation schemes do not provide benefit in the form of periodical payments. The more usual provision in these contingencies has been for a lump sum to be paid unconditionally, with no inquiry or reservation as to how it might be used, except in the case of children. A single payment of a few years' wages is markedly inferior to a pension for a worker with a lifelong disablement or for dependent survivors; but a system of periodical payments is difficult to organise on the basis of the individual employers' liability, even if it is backed by an insurance policy.

FULL COVERAGE OF EMPLOYERS AND WORKERS

Workmen's compensation approached full coverage by stages. The first schemes tended to apply to the more hazardous industries, such as heavy engineering and mining. Thereafter, a country would extend its scheme until it covered all workers in places of employment where there was a significant likelihood of injury by accident (occupational diseases raised special problems). The fringes of coverage might vary from country to country. Some might take the view that certain persons, such as outworkers who took material home to be finished or made up, or relatives working in a family business, were not strictly "employees". Some might take the view that the incidence of injury in domestic employment or on small non-mechanised farms was not significant enough to be covered by legislation. Opinions might vary on whether higher-paid non-manual staff should properly be included in a workmen's compensation law, and as a rule they would be left out.

Comprehensive social insurance programmes have approached the ideal of full coverage by a different route. For technical, administrative or financial reasons they have, in a number of countries, extended their cover either horizontally, starting with the larger urban areas, or vertically, starting with the larger employers. They, too, have had to face some of the same problems of fringe groups such as outworkers, white-collar staff, casual employees, and so on, but the tendency has been to include them wherever possible.

EMPLOYMENT INJURY INSURANCE CONTINGENCIES AND BENEFITS

In an employment injury insurance scheme, benefit is paid out of a common fund. The several consequences of the employment injury are matched by a structure of benefits, including life pensions where appropriate. The contingencies are usually differentiated in the following way:

1. *A morbid condition.* This is to be met by the provision of all necessary medical care.
2. *Interruption of earnings because of incapacity following the injury.* This is to be met by immediate periodical payments.
3. *Residual loss of physical or mental faculty.* This is to be met by a pension, or, in less serious cases, a grant.
4. *A fatal case.* This is to be met by a pension for surviving dependants.

A distinction is drawn between accidents which occur at work and diseases which owe their origin to work.

The industrial accident

The Employment Injury Benefits Convention, 1964 (No. 121), lays down that the term "industrial accident" shall be defined in the national legislation. Such a measure is unavoidable because, it is fair to say, no wholly satisfactory form of words has been devised.

Most schemes confine their attention to cases of personal injury, though some will allow expenses where an accident at work has damaged, for example, an artifical limb or other prosthetic appliance. The injury has to be accidental and unlooked for from the point of view of the injured worker, however routine, repetitive or deliberate the incident may have been from another point of view. Naturally, the accident must have occurred in the course of employment. Although there is not usually any difficulty in demonstrating this, awkward borderline cases occur when the precise point in time and place that the day's work begins or ends is in question, when accidents happen during authorised work-breaks, and so on.

It will be appreciated that, when liability for payment of compensation was placed on the employer, it was in the employer's interest to contest the claim on all points and to seek to narrow the interpretation of the industrial accident as far as possible. The manager of a social insurance fund is not under the same compulsion to test theoretical objections, but will rather tend to interpret doubtful aspects in favour of the injured worker, ensuring that not only the letter of the law but also its intention is honoured.

There are a number of ways in which the protection afforded by employment injury schemes can be liberalised and widened. One which is advocated in the Conventions and which more and more countries have adopted is the coverage of commuting accidents — that is, accidents which happen between the worker's residence and place of work. A number of countries have extended protection to cover accidents happening in the course of Red Cross activities or other rescue work, during fire brigade or special police duties, civil defence, recognised trade union activities, and so on. In exceptional cases, a national law may embrace accidental injury which occurs while the employee is acting without orders or contrary to instructions, provided that what the employee was doing was for the purpose of the employer's trade or business.

Occupational diseases

In the early days of the development of employment injury protection, attention was concentrated on accidents at work. It was only later that protection was widened to include diseases contracted during work processes. It proved difficult to define the diseases which ought properly to be within the protection of the employment injury law, while excluding common conditions which are prevalent among the general population. Usually the national legislation contains a list of diseases which are, beyond dispute, of an occupational origin, at least when they are contracted by a person who has worked in a process, or in contact with a substance, which can cause the listed disease. In 1925 the International Labour Conference was able to agree on only three diseases which could be so prescribed — lead poisoning, mercury poisoning and anthrax. But research establishes new criteria of proof, and the accelerating development of industrial chemistry and physics brings in its train new hazards. Thus, the Employment Injury Benefits Convention, 1964 (No. 121), contained a list of 15 occupational diseases and the list was further revised in 1980 to include a total of 29.

There are three ways in which national legislation arranges for the coverage of occupational diseases. Two of them are based on a prescribed list of proven and accepted diseases (similar to, but not necessarily the same as, the list in Convention No. 121) in which each disease is matched to the occupation or process in which workers are at risk of contracting the disease. Such a list creates a legal presumption in favour of a worker in the prescribed occupation; if the disease is contracted, the worker is covered, without question. In the "closed list" system, only the diseases which are prescribed are accepted, so there is an arbitrary distinction between them and others which, though they may well be of occupational origin, are outside employment injury cover. The "open list" system is similar, except that the administrative authority is given the power to add diseases to the list when experience and research have proved that a particular disease is specific to a particular occupation.

The third method is completely open. It is based on a definition which accepts the occupational origin of any disease if, by its nature and incidence, it appears to be attributable to the claimant's employment. This wide definition has the drawback that it leaves the burden of proof, at least formally, upon the injured worker. But the existence of a conventional list of accepted diseases, even though it is not incorporated in the legislation, operates in the worker's favour. It also allows claims to succeed for diseases which by their nature could not be prescribed in a list, as for example when a common infectious or contagious disease is contracted by a hospital worker engaged in combating such diseases.

Once the diagnosis has been made and it has been established that the claimant was recently employed in the defined occupation, the normal rules for benefit are applied. Instead of a "date of the accident", a "date of development" is established and is taken as the first day of incapacity due to the disease. In an employer's liability scheme it may also be necessary to look at a critical period leading up to the first day of incapacity, in order to apportion liability between two or more employers during that period.

Medical care

The medical care extended to victims of employment injuries is often more liberal than that provided as part of sickness benefit. This difference is reflected in the corresponding parts of Convention No. 102. In effect, Convention No. 102 provides that the injured worker should have every type of care, including the supply and maintenance of prosthetic appliances, the provision of eyeglasses and dental care; it sets no time-limit and envisages no cost to the worker. The later Employment Injury Benefits Convention, 1964 (No. 121), takes into account the situation in those countries in which medical care is provided under a general health service or with cost sharing by the patient, and considers that the same terms and conditions may apply in a case of employment injury, provided that there are safeguards to avoid hardship.

Interruption of earnings

The distinction between temporary and permanent incapacity which appears in most workmen's compensation law is not significant in the pattern of benefit found in employment injury insurance. Employment injury insurance recognises the incapacity for work which immediately follows the accident or development of the disease, and provides periodical payments calculated in the same way as for sickness benefit. The rate of injury benefit is by custom higher than that of sickness benefit. Convention No. 121 quotes a minimum of 60 per cent of pre-accident earnings and discourages the imposition of any waiting days; most countries pay that rate or exceed it. Some legislation requires the employer to grant paid injury leave for a few weeks, and after that the social insurance scheme takes over.

The periodical payments provided by employment injury insurance are continued during a prescribed period, usually six or 12 months. Most injuries will clear up under medical care during that time, leaving the patient no longer incapable of work. It is at this point, with the physical condition stabilised, that the aspect of residual disablement can be taken up. In a more serious case the patient's condition might not be stabilised and the patient might still be under care at the end of the prescribed period. Naturally, payment of the benefit would continue, either by a temporary extension of the injury benefit or perhaps by a provisional award of disablement benefit.

Residual loss of faculty

In their guidance for the preparation of national legislation, the Conventions speak of "loss of earning capacity likely to be permanent or corresponding loss of faculty". In practice, an attempt is not always made to ascertain the actual reduction of earning capacity in each individual case as the imponderable psychological factors and changing circumstances of the employment market make a true evaluation extremely difficult. In some countries there are tables which list items of physical injury and of loss or impairment of physical faculty (including, if the legislation so provides, disfigurement). The tables also note the degree of disablement which each item represents. As this method is a simple one, it appeals in countries where administrative and medical resources are still limited. The task of the medical assessor is to match up the claimant's condition with the corresponding item on the table, or with the nearest comparable items, and to report his findings. Sometimes the assessor is free to adjust the assessment to meet what he adjudges to be the exceptional circumstances of a particular case. In other countries, on the contrary, the assessment is required to be based strictly upon the estimated loss of earning capacity attributed to the physical disablement, taking into account pre-accident earnings and status, state of training and possibility of rehabilitation, future career prospects, and so on, and the schedule of degrees of disablement is to be used only for guidance, if at all.

The translation of the assessment of disablement into an award of benefit is usually straightforward. An assessment of 100 per cent, or total disablement, will result in a pension at the same rate as the periodical payments which commenced immediately after the injury, but lower or higher rates are found according to various policy requirements or the judgement of different legislators. If, as is more usually the case, the assessment of disablement is less than 100 per cent, any pension which is put into payment is similarly proportional to the pension for total disablement. Once again, policy requirements and judgement come into play because it is accepted and written into the Conventions that assessments of a small degree of disablement need not be turned into correspondingly meagre pensions. When there is a substantial degree of disablement, the benefit will be by way of pension; otherwise, the situation will be met by the payment of a lump sum for disablement. Schemes vary in the degree of disablement for which a minimum pension will be awarded and below which a grant will be paid; the figure chosen may be as low as 10 per cent or, in exceptional cases, as high as 30 per cent.

The award may be increased when a condition requires the constant attendance of another person; the pension may be raised by half as much again. Some schemes pay an unemployability supplement when the disablement pensioner is judged to be totally incapable of work.

We have seen that the Conventions allow a choice between loss of faculty and loss of earning power. Broadly, the one may be accepted as corresponding to the other and, on the whole, this is how it works out in practice. A minor injury, for which a grant has been paid, has little or no effect upon earning capacity, whereas a pension will buttress diminished earning capacity in more serious cases, and the worker's success as a wage earner does not usually affect the rate of the pension. Nevertheless, hardship may result, as when a small injury has a disproportionate effect upon the career prospects of a specialist worker or skilled tradesman. For this reason, in some countries in which the initial assessment is based on a table of loss of faculty, special allowances have been devised to supplement awards in particular circumstances and to enable a pension rather than a lump-sum grant to be paid.

Survivors' benefit

When a worker dies as the result of an employment injury, pensions may be paid to survivors as defined in the legislation. A funeral benefit may also be payable. As with the other employment injury benefits, there are no qualifying conditions about duration of employment or insurance, or payment of contributions.

The definition of the survivors who are entitled to benefit under the employment injury branch of a social insurance programme is usually wider than that which is laid down for survivors' benefit in the general, non-occupational, branch. Priority is given to the widow, irrespective of her age, ability to work, or responsibility for children (but usually on condition that she was living with or maintained by the deceased worker). Similar priority is accorded to a widower, but usually only if he is an invalid. (It may be noted that there is an increasing trend to abolish this discriminatory provision.) Children who were maintained in the household take second priority, and dependent parents take third priority. Some schemes may reach to a fourth priority, namely, any other dependants.

The reason for listing beneficiaries in order of priority is that not all of them could receive benefit in respect of one death. Typical rates of survivors' pension are 30 per cent of the worker's pre-accident wage for the widow; 15 per cent for each child or 20 per cent if orphaned of both parents; and 20 per cent for a parent; subject to a prescribed maximum total of, say, 75 per cent. These rates, incidentally, would satisfy the minimum level set in the Employment Injury Benefits Convention, 1964 (No. 121), which expects that a widow with two children would receive at least one-half of her husband's pre-accident earnings by way of pension.

REHABILITATION OF DISABLED PERSONS

Many social insurance programmes which provide employment injury benefits are also concerned with the rehabilitation of disabled persons. The provision of artificial limbs and other orthopaedic appliances has long been an element of employment injury medical care, but the history of comprehensive rehabilitation, that is to say, medical, vocational and social rehabilitation, is more recent. It was only after the Second World War that the rehabilitation of the disabled became an objective of major social policy in many countries of the world.

Nationally organised rehabilitation programmes may provide services for disabled persons irrespective of the origin of their disability; at the same time, social security institutions may finance medical and vocational rehabilitation facilities for persons injured at work. Some social insurance institutions have their own rehabilitation centres, the services of which are available equally to those injured at work or elsewhere. However, schemes of compensation based on employers' liability, with or without an ingredient of commercial insurance, cannot readily be adapted to provide rehabilitation facilities for the disabled.

Convention No. 102 requires the authorities responsible for medical care to co-operate wherever they can with general vocational rehabilitation services in order to re-establish handicapped persons in suitable work. The Employment Injury Benefits Convention, 1964 (No. 121), goes into greater detail and lays down that a country should "provide rehabilitation services which are designed to prepare a disabled person wherever possible for the resumption of his previous activity, or, if this is not possible, the most suitable alternative gainful activity, having regard to his aptitudes and capacity"; and should "take measures to find suitable employment for disabled persons".

Rehabilitation and benefit – a dilemma

It is possible to see a conflict in the relationship between cash benefits for permanent incapacity and the rehabilitation of the injured worker. If long-term benefit is to be regarded primarily as compensation for loss of earning capacity, should it be reduced or suspended if, after rehabilitation, the beneficiary returns to gainful employment and earns more than was anticipated when the rate of benefit was determined?

One answer to the question is based on the idea of "rehabilitation before pension", namely, that a final award of pension should not be made until every indicated measure of rehabilitation has been taken and the beneficiary's earning capacity has stabilised. Otherwise, the disabled person could well be reluctant to co-operate in measures of rehabilitation, might be tempted to postpone returning to active work or not to work at full capacity, and might not in any way assist a process which in theory would increase earning capacity but in fact would reduce benefit.

A further answer to the question is the suggestion that the long-term benefit be awarded as the sum of two elements. One element, an "impairment" benefit, would represent the irreversible loss or impairment of physical function and would be awarded for life; the other, the "disability" benefit, would be related to loss of earning capacity, which could be reviewed in the light of various factors, including the progress of rehabilitation.

PREVENTION OF EMPLOYMENT INJURY

When employer's liability schemes began to provide employment injury benefits, many people thought that one result would be a quickening of interest in industrial safety. Time has passed without any spectacular effect of this kind but, as both social security schemes and safety legislation have developed in response to economic and technological progress, a link has gradually been established between the two aspects of social policy. Benefits both in cash and in kind represent only one facet of social security policy. For the health of the individual and of society — and of the funds of the social security institution — prevention is better than cure.

Some national legislation requires the social security authority to collaborate with the agencies concerned with industrial safety, health and welfare. Elsewhere, the employment injury benefit scheme and industrial safety, health and welfare are entrusted to a single agency and, in a number of countries, the trade union movement is actively involved in their administration. Alternatively, the connection may be indirect, as when a part of the social security contribution is diverted to the financing of safety and health research.

Another advantage claimed for the workmen's compensation method of financing employment injury benefit was that an employer with a good safety record could expect to see this reflected in lower insurance premiums — the so-called "merit rating" system. Where employers' liability has been replaced by an employment injury insurance scheme, some countries have considered whether to retain merit rating, but the arguments in favour of a uniform contribution system and its administrative convenience have generally prevailed. There are other ways in which the social security authority can direct attention, and an appropriate part of its budget, towards occupational safety and health.

As a footnote to this chapter, reference can be made to two general trends which reflect the "no fault" technique originally devised for workmen's compensation and which may influence the future shape of protection against employment injury.

One trend is towards the extension of coverage beyond the category of employed persons only. Already various countries admit defined groups of self-employed persons, persons who stand on the fringe of gainful occupation, such as students and trainees, and unemployed persons while their status obliges them to attend at employment agencies. Some accident insurance schemes allow non-employed persons to register voluntarily. Such widening of coverage also calls for a modification of the definition of the relevant employment injury. A powerful impetus behind this trend towards universal protection against the consequences of injury, regardless of where the injury occurred or the employment status of the victim, is of course the rapidly increasing hazard of motor vehicle traffic.

Another route by which progress may be made towards uniformity of cover is in the reconciliation of the rates and conditions of benefit in the employment injury and the general branches of social security. In principle, the needs of an injured or disabled person are the same whether the handicap is work-related or non-occupational in its origin, or congenital.

OLD-AGE BENEFIT

7

A VARIETY OF PROVISIONS

If the objective of social security is to provide an appropriate cash benefit for the demands of a particular contingency and for the needs of a particular individual, in no branch have the planners exercised their analytical skills and ingenuity more thoroughly than in devising schemes of benefit for old age. In order to meet a variety of personal, social, financial, industrial and demographic circumstances, they have woven detailed variations into the basic pattern of the four different techniques of social security provision outlined in earlier chapters. These four techniques may be set out more fully as follows:

1. *Universal benefit schemes*. These schemes provide pensions for all residents over a specified age, irrespective of their income, employment status or resources.

2. *Universal social assistance schemes*. These schemes provide benefits for old persons who are in need, after investigation of their resources and unavoidable commitments.

3. *Social insurance schemes*. These schemes provide benefits for members in old age, subject to their record of employment or contributions.

4. *Provident funds*. A lump-sum benefit, made up of the contributions to the fund and interest, is paid out to contributors at a specified age; occasionally the lump sum may be converted into a pension.

Most such measures of old-age benefit also provide invalidity benefit and survivors' benefit.

The most useful old-age benefit, in social security terms, is a life pension. Such a pension is always granted under universal benefit schemes. A social assistance benefit, once granted, also continues for life unless the recipient acquires further resources and ceases to be in need. Established social insurance schemes are designed to pay life pensions, but members who reach the specified age without a sufficient record of employment or contributions — and this will often be the case in the early years of an insurance scheme — may receive lump-sum grants. The inadequacy of a grant, instead of a periodical payment or pension, has been mentioned in earlier comments on the provident fund technique and on workmen's compensation.

DEVELOPMENT OF BENEFIT SCHEMES

In some countries, particularly in Western industrialised countries with a long history of social security provision, the framework of social security benefits for the elderly embraces two or more separate types of scheme. Even in developing countries with more recent social insurance arrangements, there are likely to be older, means-tested, assistance schemes to protect the aged. For example, benefits available under a universal benefit scheme for all residents are often supplemented by a parallel scheme for persons in gainful activity. Some countries have introduced one centralised insurance programme, often coupled with social assistance, for all sections of the working population, whereas others have set up separate schemes according to the employment status of the workers or to the occupation in which they are engaged. Often statutory schemes have been supplemented by private pension plans initiated by joint action within the industry or by the employer. Occasionally such plans have been integrated into, or co-ordinated with, the statutory scheme, but more usually the administration of the state scheme and the private plan remain separate.

The provident fund occupies a niche of its own. It is usually established on the basis of two somewhat conflicting arguments: firstly that in a developing country the unsophisticated worker cannot be expected to appreciate the operation and superior value of a funded pension system; and secondly that the fund will be converted into a social insurance pension scheme in due course. A provident fund may undertake to buy the beneficiary an annuity instead of the lump-sum benefit and some provident funds have been redesigned as pension schemes, but in many cases the intention to convert the fund into a social insurance pension scheme is never realised. It may be that one of the secondary reasons for embarking on a provident fund arrangement — that of mobilising internal savings in aid of the national economy — obscures the consideration that a pension fund would serve that end equally well and would provide more effective social security protection at the same time.

CONTINGENCIES AND PENSIONABLE AGE

To attach benefit entitlement to the attainment of a specified age is a simple concept and the universal benefit scheme which was mentioned at the start of this chapter puts that concept into practice very simply, with only a residence condition. The earlier social insurance schemes did the same: when the contributions had been paid, the pension matured at the specified age regardless of the employment status or earnings of the recipient.

The practice of paying a pension at a specified age without qualifying conditions may be justified on the principle that, in time, everyone earns the right to rest and to take life more easily or that, as they grow older, most people naturally reach a stage when their working capacity diminishes. There are other practical considerations. When the specified age is high, the number of beneficiaries is relatively low and the administrative expense of applying means tests or retirement conditions is not worth while. Or again, it may be government policy to keep people at work and a small unconditional pension will be useful to old people without inducing them to give up their occupation. The simplest reason for adopting a universal benefit scheme is that most contributors believe that they have paid for a pension at pensionable age and should get it without irksome conditions.

Retirement

The universal social assistance scheme adds an income test to the idea of a pensionable age and certain social insurance schemes (which are designed to provide benefit in replacement of wages) insist on a retirement condition. The principle is really the same, that pension is provided at the prescribed age only if the claimant suffers a loss or a substantial reduction of income or withdraws from the labour market. Such schemes do not allow people to receive remuneration and old-age benefit concurrently. Strict application of the principle, unless the level of benefit is unusually high, could cause hardship; it might force older workers to choose between accepting an inadequate benefit, without the possibility of supplementing it by their own efforts, or continuing to work after pensionable age. And it would go against the interest of older workers who wanted to continue in light work, not so much for the income as to preserve their active participation in social life.

Between the two extremes — the unconditional pension and the absolute retirement condition — there are various intermediate arrangements. There are schemes which pay a reduced old-age benefit concurrently with wages. In a second group of schemes, title to benefit is tied to retirement from the employment or industry covered by the scheme itself. Thirdly, there are schemes in which claimants have to retire from regular employment in order to qualify for the pension, but may thereafter take casual or part-time work provided that their earnings do not exceed a prescribed amount; if their earnings exceed this amount, the pension is reduced or withdrawn. Furthermore an insurance-based scheme may allow pensioners to change their minds, cancel their retirement, return to regular employment and continue to build up an improved title to pension. Finally, there are schemes which recognise that some contributors have no wish or intention to retire at all and the retirement condition which such schemes impose at normal pension age is waived after a period to allow a pension to be paid unconditionally.

Normal pensionable age

Almost all the existing schemes provide for an age at which benefit is normally payable, if other qualifying conditions are satisfied. Strictly speaking, a "normal pensionable age" is different from a retirement age. Retirement age is the age at which workers either decide to withdraw themselves from full-time gainful activity or are obliged to leave their jobs. However, workers may not wish to retire before they have become entitled to cash benefits to support them and their dependants in their retirement life. Collective agreements or work rules may provide that the covered employees leave the establishment when they reach a fixed age, but this age is frequently the same as the normal pensionable age in the statutory scheme.

Apart from its significance to the worker, in a funded insurance scheme the normal pensionable age is of importance to the actuary whose task it is to establish the financial relationship between the income and the expenditure of the scheme.

Normal pensionable age is the same for men and women under many existing schemes, whereas others provide for different ages, the difference often being five years lower for women. The normal pensionable age under the schemes in industrialised countries is comparatively higher than in developing countries. From the figures in table 2 it can be seen that a majority of the schemes in developing countries have fixed the normal pensionable age for men at 60 or less, whereas in industrialised countries it is concentrated around 65 or more.

Experience in many countries shows that, once a normal pensionable age is determined and introduced, it is extremely difficult to change it upwards, whereas it can be lowered without much resistance. Countries which have lowered the normal pensionable age have done so in response to the growing aspiration for earlier retirement and the demand for increased employment opportunities for young unemployed persons. However, it should be noted that the lowering of the normal benefit age, for example from 65 to 60, would increase the benefit expenditure by some 50 per cent, and that in practice it might not improve employment opportunities, since business management might well wish to take advantage of the reduction in the number of older workers by reorganising

Table 2. Normal pensionable age for men in the member countries of the OECD and in selected countries in the early 1980s

Age	OECD countries [1]	Other countries [2]
50	—	1
55	1	13
57	—	1
60	3	18
65	16	7
67	4	—

[1] The 24 member countries of the OECD. [2] A selection of 40 developing countries in different regions of the world.

Source. ILO: *Income maintenance and social protection of the older person: income security for the elderly*, Report to the World Assembly on Aging, Vienna, 26 July-6 Aug. 1982 (Vienna, doc. A/CONF.113/17; mimeographed).

the enterprise, rationalising its methods of work and reducing the total pay-roll.

Health and employability

There are about 40 countries in which the pensionable age is lower for those people who have worked in conditions which are regarded as particularly arduous or unhealthy. In some cases this provision is part of a special scheme in the mining industry, the merchant marine or the railways, but it may also be found, conditionally, in schemes of general application. There are about 30 such schemes in which the pensionable age is lowered for any person who, although not positively disabled, is adjudged to be insufficiently physically fit to continue his occupation.

Such a provision closes the gap between the contingencies of old age and invalidity, a gap which is inevitable when the definition of invalidity is too strict to allow a social security benefit for a person whose health is failing with advancing years but who is yet short of normal pensionable age.

The period prior to normal pensionable age is also the time when workers are most vulnerable to the twin scourges of redundancy and extended unemployment. To cope with this, a country may modify the rules in the social security programme so that, for the long-term unemployed over a certain age, either the normal duration of unemployment benefit is extended or the normal pensionable age is brought forward.

Disability and invalidity pensioners are heavily concentrated in the older age groups. Some studies reveal a close correlation between the rate of unemployment and the incidence of long-term sickness and invalidity. When the labour market is such that it is difficult to place candidates who are fully fit and capable, the openings for older people who are rated less fit and capable are bound to be limited or non-existent. Unemployment benefit is normally reserved for those who are able to work and who are available for work. On the other hand, invalidity benefits are often confined to those who cannot undertake any gainful occupation at all. Thus, unemployed older workers who are prevented by failing powers from following their previous occupation may be left unprotected for some time after they have exhausted any title to sickness benefit and until they reach normal pensionable age. This is an area in which the social security planners have to ensure that the three systems of protection are carefully co-ordinated.

Length of service

In some countries an old-age pension can be drawn in advance a number of years before the normal age or even without regard to age if the person concerned has completed a minimum qualifying period of contributions. The qualifying period required varies from 20 to 45 years and is generally longer when the normal pensionable age is higher. This early payment of pension does not usually entail any reduction in the rate.

Voluntary early retirement

A number of social security schemes permit covered persons to claim benefit a few years in advance of the normal pensionable age if they so wish, even though they are quite fit and their job is not threatened. The reasons for doing so would be individual and personal: the length of their working career and the rates of pension already earned; the maturing of pension title in an occupational pension plan; their own assessment of job satisfaction as against planned leisure and the chance to develop some hobby; perhaps even the additional welfare advantages available to people who have officially retired. Generally, the normal age may be anticipated by up to five years, and the reduction from the normal rate of pension (on actuarial advice in a funded scheme) works out at about 5 to 7 per cent for each year.

Deferred retirement

Only occasionally in social security schemes (although more often in occupational pension plans) is any difficulty put in the way of people who wish to postpone retirement beyond the normal pensionable age. The legislation of some countries specifically authorises protected persons to defer their claim for old-age benefit and provides for the rate to be increased accordingly. When a country wants to encourage workers to remain in the productive labour force for as long as possible, the increased rates can be generous. Deferment may be unlimited or only for so many years, usually until the age of 70. Even when legislation does not expressly refer to deferment of benefit, the fact of continuing to work beyond the minimum pension age may qualify the claimant for a higher rate of pension.

Various provisions on flexible pension age, both upward and downward, as described in this section and the three preceding sections, were written into the international standards concerning older workers which were adopted by the ILO Conference in 1980 as the Older Workers Recommendation, No. 162. Recommendation No. 162 sets out in formal terms that legislation about pension ages should be as flexible as possible. This flexibility is designed to replace mandatory retirement and to permit earlier retirement, leaving the choice to individual workers. The Recommendation also contains provisions about "progressive" retirement which is dealt with in the next section.

Progressive retirement

The main difficulty which many elderly workers face is the sudden switch from active life to inactive retirement, with a consequent drop in income. Some countries have therefore introduced the possibility of reducing full-time work by stages, with a guaranteed regular income during the gradual transition from work to retirement. There is a fair amount of flexibility in the arrangements. For example, additional annual leave, paid for by the social security fund, may be granted to workers over the age of 60 or a special "partial pension" may be claimed by any worker from the age of 60 who has been transferred to part-time work. The partial pension − a percentage of the reduction in earnings − is paid until the basic pension is due at normal pensionable age. Collective agreements have been made under which an employer pays guaranteed wages during the progressive reduction in activity. Hours of work may be scaled down during the five years or so before normal pensionable age. Under another collective agreement, workers who, after more than ten years of service, have reached 60 years of age may opt to retire with 75 per cent of their wages or to continue to work part time with wages at the usual rate. All this is in line with Recommendation No. 162 which suggests that there should be a special benefit for such circumstances, secured either by legislative action or by collective agreement.

QUALIFYING PERIODS

In most countries the payment of old-age pensions is subject to the completion by the protected person of a qualifying period of contributions, employment or residence. This prevents persons who are nearing pensionable age from procuring a pension by making a nominal contribution to a social insurance scheme or, where a social assistance or universal scheme is concerned, by migrating into the country concerned. It also aims at establishing a relationship between contribution income and benefit expenditure, a relationship which will be further discussed in Chapter 12 on the financing of social security schemes.

Existing old-age benefit schemes show a considerable variety in the length of qualifying periods and their relation to the rate of the pension that will eventually be paid to a qualified claimant. It is, however, common to almost all the schemes that the qualifying period is much longer than for entitlement to invalidity or survivors' pensions. When the payment of an old-age benefit is conditional upon the satisfaction of a period of contribution or employment, the Social Security (Minimum Standards) Convention, 1952 (No. 102), and the Invalidity, Old-Age and Survivors' Benefits Convention, 1967 (No. 128), provide that a reduced benefit should normally be available when the person concerned has completed 15 years of contributions or employment. In some countries where the amount of the benefit varies according to the duration of contribution, employment or residence, no qualifying period may be required at all.

A qualifying period of at least 15 years offers no protection to those people who are approaching the pensionable age when a new scheme of old-age benefit comes into force and so it is necessary to modify the rule for them. Various devices are employed for this purpose by different national schemes. For example, there are those which graduate the qualifying period according to the individual's age when the scheme came into force. Thus, the qualifying period increases from a minimum of two or three years for older persons nearing the pensionable age to its normal length for those who are no more than middle-aged at the date when the scheme commences. In most of the countries of Eastern Europe the qualifying period is reckoned in terms of employment duration, including employment before the introduction of the scheme. This provision affords the necessary protection to most elderly workers, though it may be difficult to establish proof of employment in those past years.

The continuity and effective length of a qualifying period may be prejudiced if the employment is interrupted for any reason. The effect of such interruptions could be serious and could cause the loss of a benefit for which a person has been covered for years. Clearly, this should not be allowed to happen when the interruption is outside the covered person's control — due to sickness, injury, maternity or unemployment, the familiar short-term contingencies of social security schemes. It is the regular practice in comprehensive social security programmes for any benefit periods in the short-term branches to be credited to the claimant as if they were periods of employment or contributions, for the purpose of satisfying the qualifying periods for old-age and associated benefits.

BENEFIT

The standard form of old-age benefit is a pension, except in the case of provident funds which provide a lump sum (or, very occasionally, an annuity purchased with the lump sum) and in the case of a newly launched pension scheme which may possibly pay a grant to those elderly persons registered in it. Only fortuitously does the product of a provident fund meet the real need of beneficiaries at the time of retirement and it contributes little to their social security in old age.

Traditionally there have been two different approaches to the basic question of the level at which the pension should be paid. One such approach is to determine a general pension rate which has regard to the subsistence cost of living (or the "poverty line") in the country concerned and the other approach is to try to relate individual pension awards to the standard of living which the protected person enjoyed prior to pensionable age. Schemes which provide universal benefits, those of the social assistance type and a few social insurance schemes have adopted the former method. Most social insurance schemes have followed the latter, income-related, method. The tendency is, however, for the two to converge or to be combined. A universal benefit and an earnings-related pension are paid together in some countries and in some others the old-age pension award is made up of a flat-rate and an earnings-related component. Whatever approach is adopted, social security systems have continued to strive for a level of protection which clearly exceeds a minimum rate which would do no more than prevent actual hardship. Indeed, there is an increasing trend towards benefits which are related to the standard of living of the beneficiary. This trend naturally increases expenditure on pensions. It also increases public awareness of their cost by way of higher contributions or taxes.

Various formulae have been adopted for calculating the rate of benefit in earnings-related pension schemes. Within the confines of this chapter it is not possible to detail all the different aspects, but generally speaking the benefit starts with a basic sum which is awarded when the minimum qualifying period is completed. This sum is a percentage of the average wages, usually those received during the last five or ten years, on which contributions have been paid. If the wages for the entire period of coverage are taken into account, they are often given a weighted value to allow for the rising trend of wages in an inflationary economy.

The second element of the benefit takes into account the length of the claimant's participation in the pension scheme. It is an increment — say, 1 or 2 per cent of the average yearly wages — which is added to the basic sum for each year of participation or for each year over and above a minimum number. Many schemes then add a supplement in respect of the beneficiary's dependent spouse and children. Pensions may be made subject to a minimum and a maximum. The maximum can be established by placing a limit on the range of wages taken into account, by prescribing a maximum percentage or simply by prescribing a maximum figure. A minimum rate of pension may be defined in the same way or it may be defined as a percentage of the statutory minimum wage. Furthermore, there are schemes which discriminate in favour of lower-paid workers by applying a higher percentage at the lower end of the wages spectrum, and vice versa, when fixing the basic element of the pension rate.

It is extremely difficult, if not impossible, to compare the rates of old-age pensions provided in different countries by turning them into a common currency. Some attempts have been made, however, to indicate how much the average wage earner might expect to receive in the first year of retirement as a fraction of average earnings in the previous year. Within Convention No. 102 or the Invalidity, Old-Age and Survivors' Benefits Convention, 1967 (No. 128), it should normally be an amount of not less than 40 per cent or 45 per cent, respectively, where the person concerned has fulfilled a qualifying period of 30 years of contribution or employment or (under an assistance or universal scheme) 20 years of residence and has a spouse of pensionable age. A study carried out in the United States, covering five industrialised countries during the years 1965 to 1975 showed that the benefit level available to an average worker in a manufacturing industry, after combining the benefits from statutory social security and private pension plans, ranged from 45 to 72 per cent of previous earnings for the single beneficiary and from 62 to 82 per cent for married couples.

MAINTENANCE OF THE VALUE OF THE PENSION

Pensioners are as vulnerable as the rest of the population to the economic winds of fortune, but are less able than others to influence them or stand against them. It is not surprising that a country which institutes a pension scheme should take steps to protect its pensioners against inflation and also to ensure that they share in any general increase in the country's standard of living. Nowadays, virtually all social security administrations adjust the rates of benefit from time to time in response to variations in the economic climate.

Social insurance systems are in a special category because their funds must, for technical reasons, be reviewed by an actuary at regular intervals so as to verify that the current contribution levels are adequate to meet the cost of benefits at the current rates. The question of whether the current rates of benefit are themselves adequate is common to all social security systems and there are three ways of dealing with it:

(a) systematic or automatic adjustment, where the procedure, methods and any limits are laid down in the social security legislation;

(b) adjustment in principle, where the law requires a regular review of the rates and amounts of benefit, without specifying its method or extent, or making changes mandatory; and

(c) ad hoc adjustment, where the law contains no requirement but the authorities accept responsibility, and pensions are revised occasionally by way of ad hoc legislation.

The revision of pensions — both those already in payment and those newly awarded — is sometimes based on the movement of the national consumer price index (in order to maintain purchasing power) or sometimes on an index of wages (to reflect the movement of the average wage of the working population). A few countries make their adjustments after reference to both series of indices.

Two further aspects of the subject may be noted. Firstly, although the nature of inflationary pressures is such that the population cannot be continuously and totally insulated against them, it is widely accepted that the community has a duty to protect its older members in retirement as far as possible. Secondly, in an inflationary situation a state-wide contributory pension scheme can assume an obligation to protect its benefits, in whole or in part, from the effects of inflation. Such an obligation cannot be laid upon private occupational pension plans, though they may make such adjustments voluntarily.

SOME DEMOGRAPHIC CONSIDERATIONS

There is plenty of evidence to show that the population in many countries, particularly industrial countries, is ageing and all the projections indicate that the number of old people, both absolutely and in proportion to the population, is increasing. This process has a direct bearing on benefit schemes because it changes the balance between the active and inactive sectors of the population, the former being those whose activity supports the rest. For example, in 1950 some industrial countries had four or five persons of working age for every pensioner, but the ratio will fall below three to one by the year 2000. And in developing countries it is estimated that, during the period from 1970 to 2000, the total population will increase by 98 per cent, whereas the increase in the population of those aged 60 and over will be about 130 per cent.

In a society in which both the number of pensioners and their expectation of life are increasing, the expenditure on pensions is bound to grow and multiply, quite apart from the effects of inflation. The rise in the proportion of older people will increase the cost of medical care and of other social services and will result in greater expenditure on disability and unemployment benefits for those who are approaching pensionable age. On the other hand, in an ageing society there will be fewer workers to produce the goods and services necessary to support the dependent sectors. Many pension schemes are financed in such a way that employed and self-employed persons provide directly from their wages and profits the funds from which pensions are paid, in the expectation that future generations will do the same for them. As the ratio of active to non-active persons continues to decline, succeeding generations of pensioners must depend upon the support of a continuously shrinking workforce. Unless technical progress leads to steadily increasing productivity, the reduced workforce may only be able to shoulder the burden of looking after the elderly if they themselves, or the pensioners, accept lower standards of living.

Such a markedly uneven population growth may not be an immediate problem in developing countries, but there too the declining birth rate and increasing life expectancy will gradually have an effect. Thereafter, depending on the pace of economic and industrial progress and the development of social security policy, the planners are likely to face problems similar to those mentioned above.

Some governments have explored the possibility of raising the normal pensionable age so as to alter the ratio between old-age beneficiaries and the number of contributing (or tax-paying) workers. But, as we have already seen, this is an operation likely to encounter strong resistance.

SURVIVORS' BENEFIT

8

DEPENDENCY AND THE FAMILY

Almost instinctively, in the context of social security, one thinks of "survivors" as referring to widows and children — and of course this is very largely true. The survivors' benefit branch of social security was originally designed to meet a pattern of family life in which the married woman stayed at home, undertook the household tasks and cared for the children, while the husband and father was the provider, the breadwinner. The widow and the orphaned family were vulnerable and deprived of support when the husband died.

Gradually and increasingly the roles are changing. New life-styles are found in the community and the idea of dependency is no longer related to wife and children in the traditional sense. It is usual for both parents to be working. The mother may even be the major provider and the father an equal or major partner in child-caring tasks and in housework. The loosening of formal attitudes towards marriage means that there are more single-parent families. Thus, the social security contingencies are changing, but the changes are reflected in family benefit schemes rather than in survivors' benefit schemes which still cater primarily for the widow, the widowed mother and the orphaned children. Many schemes recognise the claims of like dependants where there was in fact no formal marriage but the parents were free to marry. Some schemes cast their protective net more widely to cover surviving dependent parents, as is common in the employment injury branch.

Although this chapter is largely concerned with the provision of benefits for widows, it is right to say at the outset that national schemes may reflect quite wide differences of culture and tradition with regard to the dependency of women within the immediate and extended family. Some aspects of these differences will be mentioned in the text.

In many countries there has been a radical change in the economic status of women during the last half century. Social security protection for the widow no longer takes the form of a simple life pension which at one time was thought to be the natural and sufficient answer to her situation.

Apart from the qualifying conditions which determine whether she comes within its protection at all, many schemes have now tailored their benefits to fit the particular circumstances of the widow — whether she is relatively young or older, has family responsibilities or not, and so on.

A provident fund is not selective in the same way. When the balance standing to the credit of the deceased husband is paid out, the relevant law may have a list of priorities, in which case the widow — unless she was separated from her husband — would almost certainly be the immediate beneficiary. The fund might, however, be bound to make the payment to another person who had been nominated in advance by the contributor.

QUALIFYING PERIODS

The Social Security (Minimum Standards) Convention, 1952 (No. 102), sets out the required qualifying periods for survivors' benefit in much the same terms as for old-age benefit but, as befits the nature of the contingency, the maximum permissible period is shorter. The effect of this is that the widow of an old-age pensioner is automatically qualified to receive a survivors' pension (subject to her own eligibility on the grounds of age or means, etc., as appropriate).

The limits established by Convention No. 102, which remain practically unchanged in the Old-Age, Invalidity and Survivors' Benefits Convention, 1967 (No. 128), are, in relation to the person on whom the claim is based, five years of contribution or employment; or three years of contribution (plus a prescribed yearly average during the whole of the working life) when all economically active persons are protected by the appropriate scheme. In practice, however, there are numerous variations on this theme, many with considerably more generous conditions attached to them.

THE WIDOW BENEFICIARY

Although the principal beneficiary of any scheme of survivors' benefit is still the widow, there are considerable variations in the way that individual schemes deal with the situation in which she finds herself. Some schemes provide the widow with a pension regardless of her age, invalidity or family responsibility. This treatment is not uncommon in countries with a tradition that women should not go out to work. Other systems give an unconditional benefit for a limited period as a transitional measure while the widow readjusts to her new status. Most schemes, however, conform in one way or another with the principles embodied in Convention No. 102 and Convention No. 128 as they apply to survivors' benefit.

National legislation is concerned not only with the civil status of the widow but also with dependency, that is with the fact that on the death of the covered person there is a loss of economic support. Clearly this can be presumed where the couple were living together at the time of the husband's death, but otherwise it will have to be spelled out in the law that there was substantial dependence or, perhaps, that the wife was dependent upon the husband to the extent of the prospective benefit. National legislation may also take into account other aspects, such as the question of polygamy in societies which practise multiple marriage or the question of a divorced survivor when the husband or wife has remarried prior to death. Legislation may even attempt to grapple with the difficult question of the priorities to be observed in such cases.

The first aspect to look at in the case of the widow beneficiary is the continuing family situation. The widow who now has care of the children of her late husband, or who is for the time being pregnant by him, should have social security support while the family grows up. Thus, there should be a pension for the mother and family benefit or special allowances for the children.

The second aspect is the widow's state of health. National legislation is invariably in line with the Conventions in providing a life pension for any widow who is an invalid, incapable of supporting herself.

The third aspect is the age of the widow. Convention No. 128 sanctions an age condition, in order that any widow not otherwise assured of a life pension will qualify if she is already over a prescribed age. In such a provision there is the suggestion of an economic reason. While a younger childless widow may be expected to take up work, the older woman is at a disadvantage in the employment market. In some schemes age figures in another rule designed to safeguard the widowed mother. If she is over a prescribed age when her youngest child grows up (that is, outgrows the definition of "a child"), the widow's pension is continued for life.

Legislation which stays close to Convention No. 128 does not provide a pension for the young, fit widow without the care of a family. This is where the transitional allowance mentioned above plays a real part in tiding the widow over until she re-establishes herself in employment. There are some schemes which arrange to pay this initial allowance in all cases, so that the widow receives a benefit from the local social security office immediately, even though in many cases it will be superseded by a pension in due course.

Social security provision for the surviving widow can rarely be neatly packaged within the survivors' benefit branch. Various elements of a comprehensive programme, notably family benefit, invalidity benefit and social assistance, are brought into play to provide the total protection which she may need.

THE CHILD BENEFICIARY

The simple definition of a child in Convention No. 102 — "a child under school-leaving age or under 15 years of age" — is sensibly expanded in Convention No. 128 to cover older children who are apprentices or students or who are physically disabled for any gainful activity.

Within the bounds of these definitions, the Conventions leave it to the national legislation to decide which children are to be recognised as dependants of the deceased breadwinner for the purpose of conferring pension title on the widow or so as to attract benefit to themselves as orphans.

When a country has a scheme of family allowances, the scheme may well define which children are to be included in the family for benefit purposes, and any such definition would carry over into the legislation for survivors' benefit. If there is no such provision, the survivors' benefit branch must have its own definition. For social security purposes it is usual to differentiate between two categories of children: issue children of the covered person (or the beneficiary, as the case may require) and maintained children. Issue children are often accepted as dependants if they were living with the covered person at the time of his death; for maintained children the conditions may be more tightly drawn. The law may require, for example, that the child had been maintained in the household of the deceased for six months before his death.

Issue children would obviously include children of the deceased covered person and the widow, and his children (if any) by a previous marriage. Since it is the family unit that is of importance, the term would also cover his stepchildren, that is, the widow's children by a previous marriage (if any).

Under some systems of law, children who are formally or informally adopted may be regarded as issue children. In yet other systems they are not so recognised. The status of illegitimate children is less well established. The general law on illegitimate children, and to a lesser degree on adopted children, may be conditioned by considerations of property and inheritance rights. Social security, on the other hand, is usually concerned with subsistence and support and often has its own rules about such children, in its own field of protection. These rules will generally be in favour of including them, if not as issue children, then under the rules about maintained children.

Many schemes set the upper age limit for a child for survivors' benefit purposes variously between 14 and 18 years. While a student, the child may be accepted for social security purposes until 18 years of age or even, in some cases, up to 27 years of age. The majority of schemes place no limit on the duration of benefit for an invalid child.

THE RATES OF BENEFIT

There are two main approaches to the calculation of the amount of a survivors' pension and these broadly follow the lines discussed in the chapter on old-age benefits. The guidance given by the Conventions is to provide a mimimum rate of benefit for a widow with two children which is the same as the old-age pension rate for a married couple and this rate should normally be guaranteed after 15 years of contribution or employment or 10 years of residence. The application of a typical formula results in the award to the widow of a pension equal to one-half of her husband's old-age or invalidity pension entitlement, and to each child, one-quarter. However, the proportions awarded vary widely from country to country. The widow's pension ranges from 40 per cent to 100 per cent of the husband's entitlement and may be fixed at different levels in the same scheme, depending upon her age and family responsibilities. Benefit payable in respect of children is fixed in the same way and may be anything from 10 per cent to 30 per cent for each child. The award may be limited to not more than a specified number of children; or the rules of the scheme may place an overriding limit on the total amount payable in respect of the one death: that limit is customarily set at 100 per cent of the husband's entitlement.

Under most programmes a distinction is made between "half-orphan" children and those who have lost both parents. The latter may be awarded up to twice as much as the former. In the case of full orphans, there will be administrative rules to ensure that the payments are used for the benefit of the children. Sometimes the award is made as a "guardian's allowance" rather than an orphan's pension as such.

One reason why it is difficult to standardise comparisons of survivors' benefit between one social security programme and another (apart from the fact that one would first have to make a comparison between their respective levels of old-age or invalidity pension) is that other family benefits, and rules for social assistance, have to be taken into account. Broadly speaking, however, when a covered person dies leaving a widow and children, his prospective right to pension is transformed into a pension and allowances for his widow and children, to assist them while the children are at school or for a period thereafter at college, or as continuing partial support should any one of them be an invalid.

OTHER BENEFICIARIES

This chapter has concentrated on benefits for the surviving widow and the children. But many schemes are prepared to extend their benefits to other surviving dependants.

In almost every case where a pension is available to a widow when her husband dies, the same pension is available to a widower when his wife dies (provided, of course, that she was covered by the social security scheme), but only if he is an invalid incapable of supporting himself. Although there is a trend away from making such distinctions between men and women, only a very small minority of schemes have as yet removed this one.

Few schemes go outside the family circle of spouse and children, probably because the amount of pension that can be sustained by a survivors' benefit scheme is limited and is best concentrated where it can have the most effect. But not all covered persons are married and some of them support other relatives who must suffer the loss of that support when the covered person dies. So a scheme may include a further list of lower priorities. The most usual further beneficiaries are aged dependent parents. Other schemes try to spread their benefits over a longer schedule of relatives, but on the whole it seems to be appreciated that it is better to identify successive priorities for benefit than to dissipate the limited amount available by sharing it too widely.

The seeds of future development can be seen more clearly in some other branches of social security benefit than in the survivors' benefit branch. However, there are two ways in which the pattern might conceivably be varied in response to social need and the changing circumstances of family life. The first would be to embrace in the scheme of benefits the adult family dependant who at present has little or no claim upon social security protection — the typical examples are the sister who acts as housekeeper to her brother or the daughter who is devoted to the care of her parents. The second would be to recognise that these days a family is most likely to be supported not by one breadwinner alone but by two in partnership and that, if the wife should die, the economic effect is no less serious than if the husband should die. The logic which has decreed a widowed mother's benefit for the family deprived of a father now argues in favour of a widowed father's benefit, on similar terms, when a family is deprived of the mother.

INVALIDITY BENEFIT

9

AFFINITY BETWEEN SICKNESS, INVALIDITY AND OLD AGE

Invalidity, as a subject for cash benefit under social security, is more often than not grouped together with old age and survivorship. Certainly the Social Security (Minimum Standards) Convention, 1952 (No. 102), laid down parallel requirements for old-age, survivors' and invalidity benefits, and 15 years later those three contingencies appeared jointly in the Invalidity, Old-Age and Survivors' Benefits Convention, 1967 (No. 128). In one sense, invalidity benefit may be regarded as an early retirement pension, granted in prescribed circumstances. In most countries the legislation is framed accordingly. Only a few countries have kept their legislation for invalidity benefit and for old-age benefit separate. There are others where invalidity is regarded rather as long-term or permanent illness, to be met by an indefinite extension of sickness benefit until this is superseded by retirement pension at normal pensionable age. Generally, however, the similarities between invalidity and old-age benefits are more significant than the differences.

Almost all statutory provident funds cater for invalidity, as well as for old age and surviving dependants, in their own fashion, paying out the balance of the member's account when invalidity is established according to the rules of the fund. Countries with a universal benefit or social assistance scheme invariably include invalidity as one of the contingencies for benefit.

The first invalidity insurance schemes for wage earners were introduced in 1889 in the old German Empire. Certain categories of workers were excluded, however, such as those earning more than a prescribed amount. Subsequently, many other countries, including some which had already set up separate schemes for defined groups of workers, legislated for employed persons generally.

The most important and probably the most difficult technical problem in this branch of social security is the definition and assessment of invalidity. More time will therefore be spent in discussing what is meant by invalidity than in describing the qualifying conditions and benefit formulae, which more or less reflect those for other long-term benefits.

DEFINITION OF INVALIDITY

From a review of various national laws it can be concluded that a distinction may be drawn between three concepts of invalidity as a social security contingency, as follows:

1. *Physical invalidity*. This means the total or partial loss of any part of the body, or of any physical or mental faculty, irrespective of the economic or occupational consequences of that loss.

2. *Occupational invalidity*. This means the loss of earning capacity resulting from the inability to follow the occupation previously exercised by the person concerned.

3. *General invalidity*. This means the loss of earning capacity resulting from the inability to take up any of the possibilities open to the person concerned in the general labour market, even those which might involve a change in occupation and possibly some sacrifice of professional or social status.

The concept of physical disability can probably be traced back to early pensions legislation designed to compensate victims of war injury. However, national schemes of invalidity benefit are more likely to use a legal formula based primarily on general invalidity — which of course does not rule out attention to physical impairment. In exceptional cases, legislation is based in principle on physical invalidity, and loss of earning capacity is taken into account only for an impairment which is not separately identified in the law.

Occupational invalidity has long been the basis of special schemes for workers in certain heavy industries and for certain white-collar workers.

Frequently, however, the legal definition used does not draw a clear line between one concept or the other, since some laws which apply the concept of general invalidity also provide that the occupational experience of the applicant must be taken into account in the assessment of the degree of invalidity. A single scheme can also be based on two concepts. For example, general invalidity may qualify a person for a full pension and occupational invalidity for a partial pension. Or the legislation may provide for general invalidity as a basic rule, but occupational invalidity in the case of a blind person over the age of 55. Another national scheme for manual workers makes a distinction between skilled or semi-skilled workers on the one hand and unskilled workers on the other; occupational invalidity is specified for the former and general invalidity for the latter. However, if the unskilled worker is over 55, the assessment of invalidity must take account of the claimant's principal activities during the 15 years prior to disablement.

Under invalidity benefit schemes in almost all countries the existence of a certain minimum degree of disability is required for entitlement to benefit. The degree required is often given as a percentage and the minimum degree conferring title to benefit varies considerably from country to country — as low as 15 per cent in one, but as high as 66.66 per cent in another. Sometimes, as will be shown later, an invalidity benefit scheme puts beneficiaries into two or more groups, according to the seriousness of their disability, and awards a full rate of disability pension, a minimum rate, and possibly one or more intermediate rates.

The concepts of occupational invalidity and general invalidity grew up before unemployment benefit schemes existed. Invalidity benefit schemes did not cater for partially disabled persons who were unemployed because of lack of demand for their labour. The ILO turned its attention to this situation and, in 1944, the International Labour Conference adopted the Income Security Recommendation (No. 67) which put forward the principle that an award of invalidity benefit should take into account the situation in the employment market. If the authorities concerned could not offer a disabled person a regular job suited to his or her disability, the person should be eligible for at least a provisional invalidity benefit. If it were likely that a course of physical or vocational rehabilitation would render the person fit for an occupation in which employment could be found, a maintenance benefit should be provided while the rehabilitation was taking place. Such provisions cover periods when the contraction in the demand for labour not only prevents those of normal working capacity from finding employment but also reduces the number of openings for disabled persons. Thus, any significant rise in the number of persons out of work usually means a consequential increase in the number of invalidity pension awards.

The incidence of invalidity is closely related to age and, in many countries, the majority of invalidity beneficiaries are in the higher age groups. For example, in one European country it was reported that, at the end of 1978, more than one-half of the population aged from 60 to 64 were in receipt of invalidity benefit. In another country some 56 per cent of the population between 50 and 64 years of age were invalidity pensioners at the end of 1979. Because many elderly persons tend to be afflicted with constitutional diseases, they apply for invalidity benefit or, when it is available as an alternative, early retirement benefit based on unfitness for work.

In a situation where the award of invalidity benefit depends upon firm proof of physical disability and a parallel unemployment benefit scheme protects only those within the active labour force — that is, persons who are capable and available — an unemployed older worker who is partially disabled or enfeebled may be left without any remedy.

This is an area in which, as can be seen in other chapters, the three contingencies of old age, unemployment and invalidity meet and interact.

ASSESSMENT OF INVALIDITY

In the assessment of invalidity for the purpose of allowing or refusing a claim, social security schemes take into account the present physical or mental condition of the applicant, as certified by a medical practitioner. Generally, the foreseeable or likely consequences of current impairments are not taken into consideration, except to assess the probable outcome of vocational rehabilitation or to fix the date for the next medical examination. In some countries, however, the possible future development of the applicant's condition if he or she continues working is a factor in the assessment of invalidity. For example, an applicant may be adjudged totally disabled if regular work would constitute a serious threat to health and may therefore be entitled to a full invalidity pension.

Age is an important factor in assessing invalidity, since the same impairments and health problems usually have more serious consequences for older than for younger people. Some national laws specifically provide that a comparison should be made between the applicant and a normal person of the same age and sex, when entitlement to benefit is being assessed. Even when the relevant law is silent on this point, age is, however, always a factor pertinent to the assessment of opportunities for vocational rehabilitation. The legal provisions in one country for manual workers aged 55 or more, and in another for older blind persons, have already been mentioned. Again, where the concept of general invalidity is the normal rule, the invalidity of an older person may be assessed by reference to what has been a regular occupation.

In deciding whether a disabled worker can take up gainful employment, the worker's home address in relation to the place of work may be critical. Some legislation specifically includes this factor in the assessment of invalidity. It is clearly important in any case, even when it is not specifically mentioned in the legislation. For example, when the law requires the awarding officer to consider how possible it actually is for the disabled person to earn an income or perform a suitable job, a job may be ruled to be unsuitable if it is located far away from where the applicant lives. In one case there was a ruling on a person whose disablement meant that he could work only part time for less than half a normal working day. It was held that, for a job to be considered suitable for such a claimant, it had to be available in the area in which he lived or sufficiently near to make daily commuting feasible. But the principle is not universally accepted and legislation may be cited in which the possibility of undertaking substantial gainful work has to be assessed regardless of whether such work currently exists in the immediate area in which the applicant lives.

The legislation of each country lays down the criteria for establishing invalidity and for assessing its degree of severity. These criteria are elaborated by legal interpretation, are surrounded by administrative requirements, and inevitably contain many non-medical elements.

Medical certification is never the sole basis for assessment except in cases of total physical invalidity. The evaluation of the applicant's aptitudes and skills, and of the real opportunities that could be opened up if vocational rehabilitation were undertaken, requires detailed knowledge of the demands of various occupations as well as an understanding of general employment problems and the current market situation. The social security institution which administers an invalidity benefit scheme must therefore employ specialists in different disciplines. In one national scheme, for example, there are special invalidity committees, each composed of five members: a doctor, a rehabilitation specialist, a labour market and vocational training specialist, a social worker and a legal expert.

The term "invalidity" usually implies a relative stability in the person's health, but nevertheless national laws often contain provisions to permit subsequent revisions of the initial assessment. Invalidity pensioners are required to notify any change in their condition which might affect their entitlement to a pension and there is often a statutory requirement for awards to be reviewed at fixed intervals — say, once a year.

QUALIFYING PERIODS

In common with old-age pensions and survivors' benefit, title to invalidity benefit is subject to a qualifying period of contributions, employment or residence on the part of the covered person. In Chapter 7 on old-age benefit the twin justifications for this qualifying condition were given: to prevent abuse of the scheme by persons who might secure a long-term benefit at short notice; and to ensure the payment of a significant "premium" (in terms of the structure of the particular scheme) before making benefit available.

Convention No. 102 and the Invalidity, Old-Age and Survivors' Benefits Convention, 1967 (No. 128), set out the same patterns of qualifying periods for invalidity as for survivors' benefit. These may be up to 15 years of contributions or employment, or ten years of residence — with at least a reduced rate available after five years of contributions, employment or residence. But when all economically active persons are covered in a contributory scheme, up to three years of contributions coupled with a prescribed yearly average of contributions during working life should secure a pension, the rate varying with that average.

Qualifying periods required by existing benefit schemes vary considerably. A few insurance schemes do not ask for a qualifying period at all but consider that the applicant's insured status at the time of being pronounced an invalid is sufficient for entitlement to benefit. In a number of other schemes the qualifying period is waived if the invalidity is the consequence of an accident (thus putting occupational and non-occupational accidents on the same footing). This is logical, because an accident, unlike the slow worsening of a disease, cannot be foreseen by the victim and there is accordingly no need for a qualifying period to certify that the person properly belongs to the group of those who are covered by insurance.

Some countries impose a simple minimum period of insurance which may be anything from six months to ten years, while others lay down a residence condition, typically three or five years. Many other countries demand a minimum amount of coverage during a specified period preceding the onset of the invalidity while in yet others the qualifying period differs according to the age of the claimant. For example, the law may require two years of residence if the claimant is under, say, 22 years of age, rising to ten years of residence for a claimant aged 35 or over.

BENEFITS

About two-thirds of the existing invalidity benefit schemes calculate the rate of benefit for total disability in the same way as for old age or retirement, or express invalidity benefit as a proportion of old-age or retirement benefit. Social insurance benefits are usually calculated by reference to periods of coverage, contributions or employment. This may, in theory at least, produce a very low rate of pension if the invalidity is established early in the claimant's insurance life. It is not unusual, therefore, for invalidity insurance schemes to prescribe a minimum benefit, either as a percentage of the insured wages or as a fixed amount.

Another way of ensuring that the younger invalid enjoys an adequate rate of benefit is to take account of the periods of coverage actually completed and then to include an additional period in the calculation. For example, the rate of benefit may be calculated as if the claimant had worked on to the age of 55, even when the period of work actually completed was shorter. Similarly, under another earnings-related invalidity pension scheme, the benefit rate is computed on the assumption that the claimant has worked until the age of 65. In yet another scheme, for employees in the private sector, invalidity pensions are calculated as if the claimant had worked in the covered employment for 20 years, even if the period of work actually completed was shorter (provided that it was not less than 9 months).

As stated earlier, most of the existing schemes use the same formula for invalidity and old-age pensions. However, reference wages or earnings usually have to be differently defined for each contingency. For example, invalidity benefit may be calculated on the basis of the claimant's average earnings over the 12 months prior to the occurrence of the contingency, but earnings are averaged over much longer periods in the calculation of old-age pensions.

In countries where the social security programme is based on social assistance principles, invalidity pensions are naturally subject to an income test. There may, however, be special concessions which allow certain means or earnings to be disregarded, particularly if the claimant is blind.

Generally, most of the supplements and increments in respect of dependants, longer period of coverage, etc., available to old-age pensioners are also paid to invalidity pensioners. Virtually all invalidity pension schemes provide a supplement for the beneficiary who needs the constant help or attendance of another person. This constant attendance supplement will usually continue in payment where the invalidity pension is converted into an old-age pension at normal pensionable age. The constant attendance supplement may be a fixed percentage, ranging from 20 per cent to 50 per cent, of the invalidity pension or it may be a fixed monetary amount. Elsewhere, the amount of the supplement may differ according to whether the invalid needs attendance occasionally, all day or continuously; or it may differ for some other reason such as family circumstances or financial situation.

In the past it was often the case that only total disability would entitle the person to benefit, but in recent years a number of countries have covered invalidity of a lesser degree, with a benefit at a lower rate than for total invalidity. A review of partial invalidity benefits emphasises the lack of uniformity of practice. In some countries benefits are paid as a proportion of the total invalidity pension, according to the percentage loss of capacity. Certain other schemes provide a uniform lower rate of benefit for partial invalidity. In one country, where 50 per cent of the reference wage is awarded if the disabled person is unable to work in any occupation at all, 30 per cent is awarded if the disabled person is capable of at least earning a wage. Another scheme may be quoted where a full pension is payable if the disabled person is completely, or almost completely, incapacitated, whereas two-thirds of the full pension is payable to a person whose disability is of a lesser degree and one-half to a person whose capacity is reduced by at least 50 per cent. In a few countries lump-sum benefits are paid when the degree of invalidity is relatively minor. One national law for employees in the private sector contains a list of specified impairments arranged in groups, with prescribed rates of pension for the more serious impairments and a lump-sum grant for the least serious impairments.

REHABILITATION

When legislation is drafted for the organisation of rehabilitation services for disabled persons, there may be one principal or co-ordinating law, under a name such as "Disabled Persons Act" or "Vocational Rehabilitation Act". As a supplement to the principal law, there may well be specific enactments aimed at the training and employment of blind persons, the education and welfare of handicapped children, special services for disabled war veterans, sheltered workshops, and so on; or there may be social security legislation which obliges the responsible authority to set up, or support, rehabilitation services. Elsewhere, the social security legislation itself constitutes the legal basis for the organisation of rehabilitation services. The subject is not necessarily brought under a central policy control in this way and in some countries provisions for the welfare and rehabilitation of disabled persons may be found in the enactments concerning national health services, social assistance, social insurance, education, housing and other policy areas.

So as to facilitate rehabilitation and to make it as effective as possible, social security legislation may authorise payments for the maintenance of beneficiaries and for various other incentives, such as special subsistence allowances during rehabilitation. Thus, for example, in one country disabled persons undergoing vocational rehabilitation are entitled to a uniform subsistence allowance, payment of their social insurance contributions, essential expenditure on material or equipment, transportation, etc., irrespective of the cause of their disability. Similar provisions are found elsewhere as part of a "Disabled Persons Community Welfare Act". In one social assistance scheme, sheltered employment allowance is paid as an alternative to invalidity pension where disabled persons take up work in approved sheltered employment.

The Invalidity, Old-Age and Survivors' Benefits Convention, 1967 (No. 128), requires that each member State which ratifies it should provide rehabilitation services which are designed to prepare disabled persons wherever possible for the resumption of their previous activity, or for the most suitable alternative gainful activity, and should take measures to further the placement of disabled persons in suitable employment. The Convention also allows for the suspension of benefit where a person, without good reason, neglects to make use of the rehabilitation services available. An earlier Recommendation adopted by the International Labour Conference, the Vocational Rehabilitation (Disabled) Recommendation, 1955 (No. 99), is devoted entirely to the subject of vocational rehabilitation. This Recommendation proposes measures, including the provision of appropriate and adequate financial assistance, to enable disabled persons to make full use of all available vocational rehabilitation services. Such provision should be made at any stage in the vocational rehabilitation process and should cover, in addition to the vocational rehabilitation services themselves, maintenance allowances; any necessary transportation expenses incurred during any period of vocational preparation for employment; and loans or grants of money for, or the supply of, the necessary tools and equipment, including any special appliances which may be needed because of a physical disablement.

UNEMPLOYMENT BENEFIT 10

THE CONTINGENCY

Unemployment, as one of the contingencies normally dealt with by social security, refers to the situation of workers who have become unemployed as a result of circumstances beyond their control and who have consequently lost their earnings. Only involuntary unemployment is covered by social security. However, the expression "involuntary unemployment" is not a simple concept. It is not always easy to draw a clear line between voluntary and involuntary unemployment and the problem of doing so will be discussed in greater detail later in the chapter. At this point it is sufficient to note that, unless strict rules are adopted and close control is exercised over potential claimants, the social security institution may find itself with a comparatively open-ended commitment and it is likely that the incentive and willingness to work of many people will be removed.

As table 1 in Chapter 1 has shown, in 1981 only 37 countries operated this branch of benefit, in comparison with 136 for employment injury benefit, 127 for old-age and associated benefits, and 67 for family benefit. Unemployment benefit schemes have found their role more often in industrialised countries with a market economy and less often in countries whose economy is dependent upon, or comprises, a large self-supporting rural and agricultural sector.

FORERUNNERS

While there is some indication that primitive forms of unemployment benefit were available to special categories of workers, such as glasswork artisans in Bohemia and lace makers in Basel, Switzerland, before the nineteenth century, the forerunners of modern schemes of unemployment benefit appear to be those run in Europe by trade unions which paid out-of-work allowances to their members.

Somewhat later than the trade union unemployment funds, employers in the larger industrialising countries also became involved in unemployment benefit schemes. Such employers had an interest in promoting a stable workforce and in conserving the acquired skills of their employees. In a typical scheme the employer would contribute to a joint fund from which payment would be made to dismissed, temporarily unemployed or partially unemployed workers. The principle underlying these schemes was that the cost of unemployment benefits had to be passed on to the consumers as part of the cost of production. Such a scheme, however, spread the risks of unemployment over a single undertaking only and failed, as in the case of trade union funds, to cover the total wage-earning population.

The weakness of these narrowly based efforts led to public action to strengthen the protection of workers. Some local governments set up unemployment insurance funds which were open to voluntary participation by workers. The first of these was established in Berne in Switzerland in 1893. However, while potentially extending their scope beyond trade union membership, these local government funds did not prove very successful because of their voluntary character, which attracted mainly workers who were customarily in unstable employment.

Other local authorities entered the field of protection indirectly by granting subsidies to private unemployment insurance funds — mainly those run by trade unions — for the purpose of increasing the benefits. The subsidies were paid annually on the basis of the benefits awarded during the preceding year. This became widely known as the "Ghent system" and its success was followed by similar municipal schemes in many European towns. Some countries developed the Ghent system on a national scale, with the financial participation of the central government.

The experience of the early voluntary unemployment benefit schemes is instructive. Their limited success indicates that the risks of unemployment could not be covered by individual establishments, but only by spreading the cost over a wider field of covered persons. And unemployment insurance which operated from the wider base of a local authority area could not be implemented on a wholly voluntary basis because of the inherent danger of adverse selection. Schemes run by trade unions were successful up to a point, but often encountered financial difficulties when supported by the members' contributions only. They were inadequate when recession struck a particular industry and were unable to cover unorganised, and unskilled, workers who were most vulnerable to the risk of unemployment. Schemes run by municipalities could cover only a limited geographical area and even a moderate setback in a small area could easily exhaust the available funds. The logical development was a nation-wide system.

The first national legislation on unemployment insurance was adopted by Norway and Denmark during the first decade of the century. This legislation set up unemployment insurance funds on the principle of voluntary participation and gave them national subsidies. Similar legislation was also introduced in other European countries during and after the First World War.

The first national law setting up unemployment insurance on a compulsory basis was passed by the United Kingdom parliament in 1911. Italy was the second country in the world to adopt a compulsory system in 1919. In the 1920s a number of European countries enacted national laws setting up compulsory insurance for unemployment benefits; and Canada and the United States did likewise in the 1930s.

Cash allowances to unemployed workers whose other means did not exceed prescribed limits — unemployment assistance — were first introduced in Luxembourg in 1921. The comprehensive social security scheme introduced in New Zealand in 1938 also provided unemployment assistance subject to an income test. A similar scheme was set up in Australia by the federal legislation of 1944.

Since then, compulsory unemployment insurance has spread to other countries although, as table 1 has shown, the number has never been large. Older schemes have been restructured from time to time and a few developing countries have made limited provision for unemployment benefit.

VARIETY OF NATIONAL APPROACHES

At present, statutory unemployment benefit schemes exist in fewer than 40 countries of the world. They may be grouped into the following three types:

1. *Compulsory unemployment insurance.* Prescribed categories of employees must participate.
2. *Subsidised voluntary unemployment insurance.* Membership is optional, except in some cases for trade union members who are required to subscribe to the union funds.
3. *Unemployment assistance.* Such assistance is financed by public funds and is subject to a means, income or earnings test.

Only five countries rely solely on unemployment assistance schemes and only three on subsidised voluntary schemes. Thus, about 30 countries administer compulsory unemployment insurance. Some of the countries which have either compulsory or voluntary insurance schemes also provide unemployment assistance to support workers who fail to qualify for insurance benefits or who have exhausted their insurance rights. Some countries have special unemployment insurance funds for defined categories of workers, such as seafarers, agricultural workers, building and construction workers and railway employees.

Many unemployment benefit schemes provide scales of benefit for workers who are not totally unemployed but whose normal hours of work have been reduced for various reasons, such as shortage of orders or of raw materials, or because of weather conditions. Furthermore, in recent years some schemes have begun to provide partial benefits to workers whose earnings are reduced as a result of work-sharing programmes. Such programmes are designed to reduce the number of persons who are wholly unemployed and have proved to be an effective means of countering the worst social effects of unemployment, of conserving working skills and, at the same time, of enabling workers to maintain social insurance cover for long-term benefits which might otherwise be jeopardised.

There are national schemes which can hardly be classified as any one of the aforementioned types. For example, there is one statutory fund, based on trade union membership fees, which pays benefits to unemployed workers, but only when more than 50 employees of an establishment, who have been employed there for at least 120 days, are discharged within a period of two months. Another scheme, jointly financed by employers and workers, provides a lump-sum benefit, which varies according to the wage class and the length of service, after at least 60 days of unemployment, provided that contributions have been paid for at least 24 months.

More familiar is the kind of legislation which obliges employers to make severance or redundancy payments to workers discharged for reasons other than misconduct. These indemnities are usually paid in a lump sum and their amount is normally related to the worker's wages and length of service with the employer. Where there is no unemployment insurance, such legislation provides a protective measure for unemployed workers. Where, however, an unemployment benefit scheme is in operation beside such legislation, there may be some confusion or controversy about the relationship between the two benefits. It can be argued that each is of an entirely different nature, with severance or redundancy pay being, in part, compensation for the loss of a job and, in part, deferred wages or compulsory savings related to the period of employment; on this basis such payments should in no way affect entitlement to social security unemployment benefits. The opposite view is that the right to severance payments and to unemployment benefit both arise from the same contingency — the loss of a job — and that the employer at least is being put to a double expense in financing payments against that contingency.

WHO IS PROTECTED?

An unemployment benefit scheme is basically designed to protect persons who are in paid employment, since it is they who are exposed to the risk of involuntary unemployment. Self-employed persons are usually outside its scope. Some schemes extend protection to all categories of wage earners and salaried employees, in both the public and private sectors, whereas others contain provisions excluding workers in specified industries or occupations.

Agricultural workers and domestic workers are the groups most frequently excluded because of the administrative difficulties involved in registration, collection of contributions, determination of earnings, and so on. On the other hand, workers whose employment is so stable as to make the coverage unnecessary are in many cases excluded — for example, permanent government servants.

Workers in casual, subsidiary, occasional or seasonal employment are often excluded from the scope of protection and, even if they are covered, they may be subject to special qualifying conditions relating to the number of contributions paid or the length of employment prior to the contingency or, as the case may be, the season of the year when they do not normally follow their employment.

Personal characteristics of individual workers can also put them outside the coverage of some national schemes of unemployment benefit. For example, persons beyond pensionable age are excluded by a number of unemployment benefit schemes, presumably because alternative social security arrangements are available to them. Some schemes also exclude members of the employer's family living in the same household.

CONDITIONS FOR PAYMENT OF BENEFIT

Compared with other branches of social security, unemployment benefits can be subject to quite complex conditions. Some of these must have been satisifed prior to the occurrence of the contingency and may be referred to as "qualifying conditions". Other conditions relate to the circumstances in which the claimant's employment was terminated, or must be satisfied at the time when benefits are being paid; these may be called "eligibility conditions". The objective of all these conditions is to ensure that the benefit is paid only to those persons who are regular members of the labour force and whose present unemployed status is without doubt involuntary.

Qualifying period

There is, of course, a qualifying period to be satisfied — length of employment or number of contributions paid or, in the case of unemployment assistance, duration of residence in the country concerned. The purpose of the qualifying period is to make certain that the claimant is properly within the scope of the scheme. The length of the period is frequently six months but, in addition, many national schemes prescribe a "reference period" during which the qualifying condition must have been satisfied — say, a qualifying period of 26 weeks of employment in the past 52 weeks.

"Leaving voluntarily"

Since unemployment benefits are intended for persons who are out of work for reasons which are beyond their own control, schemes usually look critically at the circumstances in which the claimant left the job. Take, for example, the case of a worker who left employment voluntarily. If this were to be accepted without question, every dissatisfied worker could leave and rely on social security benefit. In reality, however, it is not always easy to draw a demarcation line between voluntary and involuntary unemployment, since there is often some element of compulsion when a job is given up. Thus, almost all the schemes of unemployment benefits impose a disqualification for an appropriate period when a person leaves employment voluntarily "without good, or just, cause". The application of such a provision is not always easy, and there are many judicial and administrative precedents in different countries about the construction of the term "good or just cause". For example, is a worker justified in leaving employment to take care of a sick child; because of unsafe or unhealthy working conditions; or as a result of unfriendly treatment by fellow workers?

Misconduct

The second problem to consider is that of the discharge of a worker for alleged misconduct. Many unemployment benefit schemes disqualify a worker from receiving benefit for an appropriate period after dismissal by the employer on the grounds of misconduct. However, exactly what acts should be considered as misconduct always remains a difficult question. Labour legislation in many countries provides certain guidelines for the adjudication of justifiable and unjustifiable dismissal (some legislation uses the term "industrial misconduct" to make the grounds of this disqualification narrower and more specific) and the following are generally regarded as misconduct for the purpose of disqualification: theft, dishonesty, intoxication while at work, wilful disobedience of orders or rules, frequent unjustified absence from work, excessive bad timekeeping and repeated negligence.

Industrial action

The third problem is that of labour disputes, or industrial action. If unemployment benefits were made available to workers who went on strike, their position would be considerably strengthened in relation to the employer. It would not be proper for a social security scheme to play such a one-sided role in industrial disputes; social security has to be as neutral as possible in industrial relations. Presumably for these reasons, under many unemployment benefit schemes unemployment as a direct consequence of participation in a labour dispute disqualifies a worker from receipt of benefit. A number of problems arise, however, in the application of these provisions. For example, the relation of a particular worker to a dispute may be questioned. Or again, some workers may become unemployed as a result of a dispute, even if they are not directly involved in it. The existing national practice varies to a great extent on this particular point. The Unemployment Provision Convention, 1934 (No. 44), covers the possibility of disqualifying workers from receipt of benefit for an appropriate period if they have lost their employment as a direct result of a stoppage of work due to a trade dispute; the Social Security (Minimum Standards) Convention, 1952 (No. 102), allows member States to suspend the payment of benefit.

"Capable, available and willing"

Many workers find themselves out of work because of sickness, maternity, invalidity or old age and protection is available to such persons under other benefit branches of social security. Unemployment benefit schemes, on the other hand, protect persons who are still in the labour force and invariably require the awarding or adjudicating authority to be satisfied that the claimant is capable of work, available for work, willing to work, or registered at an employment exchange office − that the claimant is, in short, part of the active labour force.

Whether or not a person is "capable of work" may be verified when a claimant reports to an employment exchange office or to any other agency handling claims under the scheme. The agency may have the power to require the claimant to undergo a medical examination. If found to be incapable of work, the claimant may transfer to the appropriate branch of the social security programme. However, persons whose working capacity is limited but who are nevertheless capable of working efficiently in ordinary employment ought not to be refused unemployment benefit. The office which handles the claims has to work closely with the sickness, invalidity, old-age and employment injury benefit authorities, as well as with the vocational rehabilitation services. It is also usually combined with the placement services.

The term "availability for work" is a broad one and the application of this condition is not always simple. A claimant must not only be in need of a job but must also be free to take one and must not, for example, be currently occupied as an independent worker, be out of reach or have only a few hours a day to spare for employment. Again, a claimant may be ruled "not available" when personal circumstances prevent acceptance of the job offered by the employment exchange office. For example, a person who can report regularly to the employment exchange may be prevented from accepting an offer of suitable employment because of having to care for an invalid or a child at home.

"Willingness to work" is tested by offering a suitable job. If suitable jobs are readily available, it is not difficult to test this condition, but when job opportunities are scarce, willingness to work cannot be verified in this way. It might, however, be considered that regular reporting at an employment exchange office is sufficient for a claimant to prove willingness to work. Sometimes the law requires this in any case.

The condition that a claimant should be "seeking work" — taking reasonable steps to find a new job — is rather moral in character because it is difficult to verify whether or not an individual person is really seeking a job in addition to reporting regularly to the employment exchange office. The real intention underlying this condition is not to allow the claimant merely to sit and wait until a new job becomes available.

Suitability of job

The question of what is a suitable job in any particular case is also difficult to answer. The fear of disqualification may induce a claimant to accept a job which, while it may seem suitable in the opinion of the one who offers it, is not so in fact. Elements to be taken into account in deciding "suitability" include wage rates, hours of work and other working conditions; location of the establishment in which the job is offered and the possibility of being reimbursed for additional travel or removal expenses; social security coverage; safety and health conditions at the place of work; and industrial relations, notably trade union membership and the presence of any labour disputes.

More generally, in administering this matter of "suitable employment", the benefit office will have regard to the claimant's age; status and length of experience in the previous occupation; how long the unemployment has lasted; the state of the labour market; and the repercussions which the offered job may have upon the personal and family life of the claimant. The situation is seldom clear-cut. A job that is suitable for a young worker may be one that an older worker could justifiably refuse, and vice versa. A person newly out of work can set stricter standards as to what is suitable than one who has been unemployed for some months.

BENEFIT RATES AND DURATION

The most commonly observed rates of unemployment benefit are 50 to 60 per cent of a claimant's previous earnings, within a maximum and a minimum. In exceptional cases insurance benefit may be at a flat rate and this is usual in unemployment assistance schemes. Most schemes add a supplement for a dependent wife and children. In about one-third of the countries which cover unemployment, the rate of benefit is the same as that for sickness. Convention No. 102 equates unemployment benefit with sickness benefit — at least 45 per cent of the claimant's previous earnings (for a man with a wife and two children), taking family allowances into account; or that same proportion of an unskilled worker's wage where it is a flat-rate benefit, again taking family allowance into account.

It is in the fixing of the maximum duration of benefit that considerable variations occur from one country to another. A small number of schemes, including some of those based on social insurance, pay benefit without limit of time. Where a limit is prescribed, it may be fixed in either of two ways. The first is for there to be a common duration of benefit for all qualified claimants, irrespective of their past employment or contribution record; the second is for the duration of benefit to vary from one person to another, according to the number of contributions paid, or the length of the past employment. There are also some schemes which make exceptions to the prescribed limit, according to the age or family responsibilities of the claimant or the state of the national economy. Convention No. 102 expects that an insurance-based benefit should be paid to a qualified person for at least 13 weeks in the course of one year, or social assistance for at least 26 weeks.

Almost all unemployment benefit schemes prescribe initial waiting days between the last day of employment and the first day for which benefit is paid. This is done to lighten the administrative and financial burden caused by frequent short spells of unemployment and because the employment exchange office may be able to place the claimant in a suitable job during that time. Most waiting periods are three to seven days. Convention No. 102 allows a waiting period of up to seven days. As with sickness benefit, the waiting days may be waived if a spell of unemployment starts very soon after a previous spell ends.

The first charge upon the funds of any scheme of unemployment benefit is, naturally, the payment of benefit to the covered persons, together with their dependants, during the period of unemployment. Many schemes also involve themselves in the positive side of meeting the contingency — paying benefits to persons who undertake industrial training or retraining; or making grants to promote measures which are designed to reduce or prevent unemployment. In addition, where the structure of the social security programme makes this desirable, the unemployment benefit fund may pay the claimant's contributions to other branches of the programme so as to maintain the person's rights, in particular the person's right to pensions benefits. (More commonly, the unemployment benefit branch is closely integrated with the other branches of social security, and the claimant's contribution record is credited with weeks of proved unemployment as if they were weeks of contribution or employment for the purpose of long-term benefits.)

FUNCTIONS OF AN EMPLOYMENT EXCHANGE SERVICE

An employment exchange service, like a medical service, has to restore the ability of its clients to be self-supporting. Before a cash benefit can be drawn, an unemployed person must report to the local employment office, giving details of his or her occupational history. The office compares the person's qualifications with the vacancies reported to it by employers and, as soon as a vacancy that seems suitable occurs, it sends the claimant to the employer for an interview. The claimant must attend at the office at regular intervals in order to learn whether a suitable job has become available. It is the office that certifies from time to time that the unemployment is genuine for the purpose of obtaining benefit or continuing to receive it.

In sickness benefit schemes, when a claimant has been certified as incapacitated for work by a medical examiner, the administrative official of a social security institution has only a limited discretion to accept or reject the genuineness of the incapacity. For unemployment benefit, however, no comparable mechanism exists to provide an independent professional or technical opinion as to the claimant's eligibility. Only questioning by skilled interviewers can bring out the facts. The various problems which have been discussed above must be resolved on the basis of the questioning and judgement of the interviewing officials at local employment offices, who must use every piece of evidence which is available and relevant. These questions concern matters of vital importance, not only for unemployed people and their families, but also for fellow workers, employers and the country's labour standards, policies and practice.

RECENT TRENDS AND PROBLEMS

Unemployment benefit schemes were originally designed to protect workers who were already members of the labour force, but not persons who had never been employed. In recent years, however, some countries have extended the scope of protection to those who have never been employed, in particular, those who have just left school or college and cannot find work. Some countries have initiated special arrangements to

Table 3. Total social security benefit and unemployment benefit expenditure in selected
countries, 1971 to 1977
(in millions of national currency units and indices, 1971 = 100)

Country	Total social security benefit expenditure		Unemployment benefit expenditure	
	1971	1977	1971	1977
Australia	2 902.4	12 449.2		618.2
(dollars)	(100)	(429)	(100)	(5 724)
Austria	74 897	159 180	1 630	4 093
(schillings)	(100)	(213)	(100)	(251)
Belgium	238 299.9	672 658.5	9 845.1	73 407.4
(francs)	(100)	(282)	(100)	(745)
Federal Republic of Germany	123 590	268 525	3 266	11 027
(marks)	(100)	(217)	(100)	(338)
Norway	14 399.2	36 402.7	138.0	432.4
(crowns)	(100)	(253)	(100)	(313)
United States	105 509	244 488	5 780	13 851
(dollars)	(100)	(232)	(100)	(240)

Source. ILO: *The Cost of Social Security: Eighth International Inquiry, 1967-1971*, Basic Tables 1976 (Geneva, 1976); ILO:
The Cost of Social Security: Tenth International Inquiry, 1975-1977, Basic Tables 1981 (Geneva, 1981).

cover self-employed persons who lose their livelihood in an economic
depression.

These developments naturally increase expenditure on unemployment benefits, the cost of which has risen sharply because of high rates of
unemployment in industrialised countries with a market economy.
Table 3 shows the rise in unemployment benefit expenditure and in total
expenditure on social security benefits from 1971 to 1977. In every case
the former increased at a faster rate than the latter and took an increased
share of the total benefit expenditure. Such statistics naturally raise the
question of whether more of the resources should be devoted to positive
measures of job creation and training — the other side of the
unemployment benefit coin.

National and international studies demonstrate that, when older
persons become unemployed, their prospects of work lessen as the
duration of their unemployment is prolonged. So some unemployment
benefit schemes lengthen the statutory period for them; elsewhere, early
retirement pensions are paid, anticipating the normal pensionable age.
Some countries have envisaged lowering the retirement or pensionable
age, or making early retirement easier, so as to expand job opportunities
for younger workers. Experience shows, however, that such policies do not

necessarily generate as much employment as may have been expected. Where such arrangements are taken up on any scale, they will also markedly increase the cost of old-age or retirement benefit.

In recent years some unemployment benefit funds have been used as the vehicle for special measures to prevent or minimise redundancy and unemployment. Such measures may be designed to encourage occupational and geographical mobility of workers or to encourage recruitment by subsidising the wages of trainees. Financial aids may be given to those who employ the disabled, the elderly or school-leavers. Sometimes grants may be made available to employers in order to minimise staff retrenchment brought about by adverse trading conditions. These aids may be financed by special contributions collected from employers through the unemployment insurance scheme.

DEVELOPING COUNTRIES

In developing countries the promotion of employment is the overriding priority in the allocation of resources for social policies and, with rare exceptions, national social security systems are not ready to move into the provision of unemployment benefits. Before an unemployment benefit scheme is launched, the employment market must be properly organised and a network of efficient employment exchange offices established. In recent years several developing countries have opened a debate as to whether or not some form of income security should be envisaged, particularly for involuntary unemployment among workers in the organised industrial sector which is now being built up. While such a discussion is fully justified, some questions are bound to be raised, such as, for example, the priority to be attributed to this sort of protection for workers in the organised sector, on the one hand, and to the needs of their families in the rural and unorganised sectors, on the other. One thing is certain: there would have to be strict controls on the coverage of the scheme and this might include control of the movement of people between the rural and industrialised areas — a measure which it is not easy to envisage.

Without strict controls, and even in the absence of any deliberate abuse of the system, any realistic programme of unemployment benefit could easily outrun the resources of a contributory scheme. The result would be either that the amount and duration of the benefit would have to be restricted and would no longer be appropriate for its original purpose, or that pressure would build up for a subsidy out of general revenue, which could well be seen as a distortion of social priorities.

FAMILY BENEFIT

11

WAGES AND FAMILIES

Family allowances, as a component of a social security programme, rest upon a foundation distinct from that of other cash benefits. Other benefit schemes stand ready to provide a guaranteed income against the day when regular wages are interrupted or are relinquished in old age. Family allowances, by contrast, recognise that the rates of regular wages in payment do not, as a rule, take into account the size of the family to be supported by the wage. And, although children's allowances and family benefit schemes are now well established in the industrial world and are frequently found in the developing countries, they were introduced to social security later than the other branches, in response to gradual social pressures, rather than to specific occurrences such as illness, injury or maternity. The social pressures included the realisation, from the early days of industrial change, that large families and poverty often went hand in hand; the experience, particularly during the First and Second World Wars, of rates of service pay which included allowances for dependants; the apprehension by industrialists that pressure for higher wages to meet family budgets might unduly inflate general wage costs; the fears expressed in some quarters that the expense of raising children might result in a decrease of population; and the experience of social security administrators themselves, who found that rates of benefit, with increases for dependants, could be higher than the wages they were designed to replace.

While the direct provision of family allowances as a social security benefit was developing, other social reforms were going ahead which paid increasing attention to the welfare of children. Free education was supplemented by subsidised meals and school medical services. Priority was given to families with children in the allocation of subsidised housing. In the fiscal sphere, income tax abatements eased the burden on the family breadwinner. With these and other advantages accorded here and there, the subject was brought under the general heading of family benefit instead of family or children's allowances.

THE ILO AND FAMILY BENEFIT

The first ILO instrument to deal directly with family benefit was the Income Security Recommendation, 1944 (No. 67). The Recommendation accepts as a guiding principle that "society should normally co-operate with parents through general measures of assistance designed to secure the well-being of dependent children" and urges the provision not only of children's allowances but also of benefits in kind, such as free or subsidised infant food or school meals, or below-cost housing for families with a number of children.

Although children's allowances are seen as a form of social assistance (rather than a benefit guaranteed by a social insurance fund), the Recommendation makes it clear that they should be paid at fixed-scale rates, irrespective of the parents' income, and should make a substantial contribution towards the cost of maintaining a child, with higher rates for older children. Allowances should be given for all children, except those otherwise provided for under a social insurance scheme, say as orphans or as dependants when a parent is for the time being drawing an insurance benefit.

It has been suggested that, while there is no positive difference of emphasis, paragraphs in the Recommendation show a preference for benefits in kind when the object is the healthy nurture of children and for cash allowances when the end in view is the support of large families. However that may be — and certainly some schemes in the 1930s were prompted by adverse movements of birth rates — there is no evidence to show that family allowances have by themselves had any marked influence on population trends. Rather have they served to diminish the difference in the standard of living between homes with young children and those without and to promote equality of opportunity in life among children.

When, in 1952, the Recommendation was codified in the Social Security (Minimum Standards) Convention (No. 102), the contingency was stated quite simply as "responsibility for the maintenance of children". In the Convention a short qualifying period was allowed for; depending upon the nature of the governing legislation, this should be not more than three months of contributions or employment or 12 months of residence. A few further elements were added to the benefit package, which might now comprise either, or both, of the following:

(a) a periodical payment to the responsible persons; and

(b) the provision of food, clothing, housing, holidays, or domestic help, for the children.

This combination of cash and services means, of course, that the minimum rate of children's allowances cannot be defined in the same way as the rate of other social security benefits. The ratifying country is asked to ensure that a minimum total amount is devoted to family benefits. Where the national legislation has a limited coverage, the Convention asks for 3 per cent of an unskilled worker's wage, multiplied by the total number of children covered; where the scheme extends to all residents, the figure asked for is 1.5 per cent of that wage, multiplied by the total number of their children.

EMPLOYMENT-RELATED FAMILY ALLOWANCES

The first organised schemes of family allowances were found in industry and commerce and in the early 1920s. When a general demand was building up for higher wages, industrialists in France and Belgium decided to meet the demand by giving special allowances to employees proportional to the number of children dependent on them. In order to prevent an undue charge falling upon any one employer, and to obviate discrimination against work applicants with large families, the employers organised "equalisation funds" to ensure that the cost per employee was evened out. It is evident that this device, repeated for separate industries or regions, or extended to the field of employment as a whole, is an application of the insurance principle, like the employers' mutual funds which may be found in the administration of workmen's compensation.

Of the 67 countries which operated schemes of family allowances in 1981 (see table 1, Chapter 1), some two-thirds used variants of this insurance-based system. Most commonly the allowances (at a flat rate for each qualifying child) are paid directly by the employers, who then settle their account with the institution which supervises the scheme and manages the equalisation fund. Although the right to benefit is conditional upon the recipient's being an employee within the scope of the scheme, entitlement is maintained in cases of sickness, unemployment, long-term disablement or retirement. On the death of an employee, the allowances may continue, or may be superseded under a survivors' benefit scheme. Having started as a private arrangement, employment-related family allowances have in general been brought under the same sort of statutory control and supervision as other branches of social security. Where coverage of employed persons has been achieved, some countries have enacted similar provisions for independent workers. In such cases the whole programme, financed by employers and self-employed persons, possibly with a subvention from general revenue or earmarked taxes, and administered by a statutory authority, attains almost as comprehensive a character as the alternative public service schemes.

PUBLIC SERVICE FAMILY ALLOWANCES

Family allowance schemes of the public service type originated in New Zealand in 1926. At first the allowances were confined to low-income families, but that limitation was soon dropped. By 1981 some 16 countries had established universal schemes of this kind, available to all parents as a general rule and financed out of taxation. As with other publicly financed social security benefits there is no direct link with employment. The main qualification is that the parent should satisfy a residence test, say of 12 months' duration, in the country concerned, or perhaps a longer period if the parent was born abroad or is not a national of the country (a similar condition may be imposed on a child). Most universal schemes specify that the allowance belongs to, or is at any rate payable to, the mother — so emphasising that it is granted in aid of the domestic expenses in the family budget — and usually the amount of the allowance increases for the second and each subsequent qualifying child.

COMPOSITION OF THE FAMILY

Family benefit is primarily concerned with the immediate family group of parents and children. The definition of a child depends on parentage, age, schooling or further education, and sometimes invalidity; and the inclusion of a child in one family group rather than another may depend on parentage, residence or maintenance. Some countries extend the family group in other ways to include certain adults.

Children

Which children count for the purpose of family allowances? The civil law of the country, and whether or not there is a civil registration system, will condition the answer to this, but normally one would expect to include issue children and step-children of the parents (or parent, as the case may be), though there may be rules to exclude a child who is neither living in the family nor maintained by the claimant. Legally adopted children normally take the full status of issue children. The status of illegitimate children may have to be specially defined for the purpose of the family benefit law.

The scheme may extend the family to include younger brothers and sisters or grandchildren of the claimant, or there may be a general rule by which any child other than an issue child may be counted as one of the family if the child lives there, under the parental care of the claimant and spouse. Naturally, the law would be so framed that a child could not be included in two families at the same time, once as an issue child of the parents, and once as an "other" child living elsewhere.

The age and ranking of the child may be important. It was not unusual at one time for public service schemes to exclude the first one or two children, on the argument that normal family income should be sufficient to meet this cost and that state support for all children would undermine parental responsibility. Few schemes have held to this line; most follow the ILO Recommendation and Convention, paying for each child. Most public service schemes make a progressive payment — so much for the first child, more for the second, and so on — but employer-based schemes which are financed on an "equalisation" basis usually do not differentiate in this way. On the other hand, there are a number of countries in which the allowance per child diminishes, or ceases altogether, beyond a certain number of children. The reason for this may be that the country concerned is pursuing a population policy and is therefore linking together family planning measures and family allowance measures.

Age is of course crucial. The upper age limit for benefit may be fixed in relation to the school-leaving age or the labour laws; this would usually put it at 14 to 16 years but very occasionally it may be younger. The standard age may be extended if the child continues in further education or vocational training, or if the child enters apprenticeship; in some countries a student retains the status of a child for this purpose until the age of 27. Where a handicapped child becomes a permanent invalid, benefit will continue beyond the standard age — either the age limit will be waived in the family benefit branch, or the child will be transferred to a parallel programme of invalidity benefit.

Adults

Some countries include adults in the award, making the scheme one of family allowances in fact as well as in name. The most usual addition is for the wife, provided that she is not engaged in paid employment, or more generally the non-working spouse. One scheme includes the unemployed young person, up to the age of 25, when the person is replacing the parent at home. Other schemes might cater for the widowed mother and aged or invalid parents or grandparents — but such a provision in the family benefit branch clearly becomes less important as other branches of a comprehensive social security programme are developed.

INCOME TAX

It has been customary in countries which levy a direct tax on personal incomes for the income tax code to allow deductions from the gross income in respect of children before the tax is assessed. Broadly, the object is to redistribute tax liability (in effect to redistribute income) in favour of taxpayers with family commitments. But a reduction of taxable income is an imperfect instrument of social justice: families whose income is too low to be caught in the taxation net derive no benefit at all; families in the middle-income groups attract a certain level of benefit; and, because income tax rates are in general progressive, families with the highest taxable incomes profit most from the arrangement. The effect of a universal scheme of family allowances is to redistribute income in favour of families with children in such a way that, regardless of income, each family of the same size enjoys the same support from the community. It has been noted that early attempts to make eligibility for those allowances subject to a means test were in general discontinued; but some countries have sought to attain a comparable effect by treating the allowances as taxable income.

A country could thus find itself paying out a family allowance to a resident, recovering part of the family allowance by directly taxing it, and then excusing the resident from paying an even larger portion of tax by way of children's credits. It may well be concluded that social justice, simplicity of administration and a logical and uniform scale of state assistance to families are better achieved by relying on social security provision. This entails paying appropriate rates of family allowance, not subjecting the allowance to income tax and discontinuing the older schemes of child allowances in the income tax system. In recent years, several countries have reviewed their programmes and recast their tax and family allowance provisions in this way.

OTHER FAMILY BENEFITS

Just as a parallel can be drawn between the definition of a child in family benefit law and in survivors' benefit law — and family benefit schemes can be used as a means of providing invalidity benefit for persons who are disabled from their youth up — so, too, are there obvious affinities between family benefit and maternity benefit. There appears to be a growing tendency to use the conventional provisions of the social insurance scheme to provide the wage-substitution benefit — the 12 or more weeks of maternity allowance — while using family benefit legislation to develop other lines of action more positively aimed at the health and welfare of the expected baby and the nursing mother.

In France, and in the African countries which are heir to the French pattern of social security, family benefits will be found to include a pre-natal grant, paid by instalments during the pregnancy, and a substantial birth grant, paid by instalments after the confinement. These payments are usually conditional upon the mother's attendance at pre-natal and post-natal medical examinations.

A rapid survey of a number of family benefit programmes brings other interesting features to light. A programme may pay a marriage grant for the newly formed family. At least one South American country pays a monthly housing allowance (at about the same rate as a family allowance for one child) to each married couple or single householder. Other countries diversify the family allowance itself. Particular care is given to the disabled child. Apart from the indefinite extension of family benefit which has already been mentioned, the normal rate of allowance may be increased or doubled, or supplemented by a special "handicapped child's allowance". In Ireland the family benefit programme comes to the aid of triplets with an exceptional lump-sum grant; half as much again is paid in the case of quadruplets. There is more than one instance in which a supplementary allowance is provided for families headed by a single wage earner. Elsewhere a "vacation bonus" equal to one month's normal family allowance is found.

Family benefit is clearly an area in which fresh ideas and new departures are to be found. For instance, in one country in the mid-1970s a conventional maternity insurance scheme was replaced by a new programme of "parental insurance". One of the incidental objects of the programme was to promote the equality of the sexes and amongst its features are the following:

1. The familiar maternity allowance is replaced by a parents' allowance, payable to either or both parents for a total of 180 days.

2. A child-care allowance is provided for a parent who has to leave work temporarily to look after a child under the age of 12 — either because the child or the regular child-minder is ill or because the child has to attend a child-care centre for preventive treatment. The benefit may be claimed for up to 60 days a year.

3. There is a system of care allowances, at the same rate as invalidity pension, to compensate parents for the additional burden of looking after disabled children under the age of 16.

Of the various ideas which are emerging from this common ground between maternity and family benefits, the idea of a child-care allowance is being more widely adopted than many of the others. It occurs in the programme of a country which has a conventional pattern of maternity allowance, with its own variations. The allowance is payable not only when a child is born, but when a child is adopted into the family. Substantial pre-natal and maternity grants are made, conditional upon attendance at mother-and-child clinics. In addition, the mother is entitled to a child-care allowance if she stays at home to care for the child until it is 3 years old; alternatively, she may be allowed paid sick leave for up to 60 days a year if a child under 3 is ill, or up to 30 days while the child is over 3 and under 6 years old. In other schemes this "sick child paid leave" is available to either parent, within the total number of days provided for.

BENEFITS IN KIND

A social security institution, particularly one with a network of local offices (such as is described in Chapter 14), may play a useful part in administering family benefits in kind — in particular medical care benefits for expectant and nursing mothers and pre-school children, and the distribution of special foods and dietary supplements. Grants and allowances for housing and vacations have been mentioned, but the physical provision of "food, clothing, housing, holidays or domestic help" for children, which are listed in Convention No. 102, would ordinarily be organised through the other programmes of a government which adopted family benefit as one branch of its social security programme.

Free or subsidised milk and midday meals are commonly part of the schools programmes, as are assisted holidays. Housing policies may make special concessions for large families or for single-parent families. Labour laws may incorporate welfare facilities for working mothers with young children. Although these matters, and the methods by which they are organised and financed, may be formally within the scope of family benefit, a discussion of them would go beyond the scope of this book.

RATE OF ALLOWANCES: SOME COMPARISONS

It is difficult to draw comparisons between the effective value of family allowances in one country and another as there are too many variable factors, such as relative costs of living, real rates of exchange, the extent to which benefit rates are biased towards older children and students and how far the amount of cash benefit is balanced by the amount of benefit in kind. It has been shown that, as a general rule, when the financing of a scheme is employment-related, the allowances tend to be at a flat rate for each child — and these rates may emerge from the local process of wage determination. In universal schemes financed from general revenue, the rate per child almost always varies according to age and ranking in the family; the same is true of employment-related systems which have attained universal coverage under a unified, state-wide management. Table 4 (derived from information published by the United States Social Security Administration) illustrates what happens in a dozen countries where the rates vary only with the number of children in the family.

Typical of most of these countries is the payment of a modest allowance on the birth of the first child, followed by a larger allowance on the birth of the second and third children, and possibly the fourth. Thereafter, the amount paid on the birth of subsequent children may be fixed or may increase only slightly. However, two countries (B and M) stand out with a scale which decreases markedly, probably because the

Table 4. Progressive rates of family allowances (universal coverage schemes) in selected countries in 1981

Child	(a) Employment-related financing						(b) General revenue financing					
	A	B	C	D	E	F	G	H	J	K	L	M
First	0.00	1.00 [1]	1.00	1.00	0.00	1.00	1.00	1.0	1.0	1.00	1.00	1.00
Second	1.00	1.66	2.79	2.50	1.00	1.00	1.43	2.4	1.0	1.56	1.33	0.79
Third	2.08	3.00	3.57	2.97	0.67	1.17	1.71	4.8	2.5	1.56	1.71	0.50
Fourth	2.08	0.33	3.00	5.88	0.67	1.33	1.71	4.8	3.0	1.56	1.81	0.10
Fifth	2.40	0.33	2.14	3.13	0.64	1.33	2.00	4.8	3.5	1.56	1.92	0.10
Sixth	2.40	0.33	2.14	3.13	0.64	1.33	2.00	4.8	3.5	1.56	1.92	0.10

[1] The rate for the first child to qualify for benefit is represented by a 1.

Source. United States Department of Health and Human Services, Social Security Administration: *Social security programs throughout the world, 1981*, Research Report No. 58 (Washington, DC, Government Printing Office, 1981).

Table 5. Average value of allowances per child in the family (universal coverage schemes) in selected countries in 1981

Number of children	(a) Employment-related financing						(b) General revenue financing					
	A	B	C	D	E	F	G	H	J	K	L	M
One	0	100 [1]	100	100	0	100	100	100	100	100	100	100
Two	100	133	189	175	100	100	121	170	100	128	116	90
Three	206	187	245	220	112	105	138	274	150	137	165	76
Four	258	153	259	313	117	113	146	324	190	142	169	60
Five	302	127	250	313	120	117	157	356	220	144	174	50
Six	332	113	244	313	120	120	164	376	240	146	212	43

[1] The average value when the allowance first goes into payment is represented by 100.

Source. As for table 4.

rates are set according to population policy as well as social security policy.

Such scales are designed not for individual children but for the family as a whole. Table 5 shows, for the same 12 countries, how the average value of the allowance per child varies as the family increases in size.

From table 5 it can be seen how the growth of the allowance as a whole shows a smoother progression than the increments for individual children might suggest. (Once again the exceptional cases B and M emphasise the general rule.) Obviously a scale like this recognises that the expense of rearing a family increases as the family grows up; another way of acknowledging this is to have a simpler basic scale and to add to it special allowances related to age — when the child reaches (say) 6, 12 and 18 years of age.

FINANCING OF SOCIAL SECURITY SCHEMES 12

ENDS AND MEANS

No social security scheme will deserve its name unless there is a reasonable certainty that the promised benefits will be paid as they fall due. The methods of financing the proposed benefits must be thoroughly studied, and a viable solution found, before the scheme is promulgated. This applies equally to statutory and non-statutory schemes; the authority responsible for any scheme, having willed the end, must provide the ways and means.

The cost of a social security scheme is the amount needed to pay for the benefits and for the expenses of administration. The amount will vary from year to year depending upon various factors which will be analysed later in this chapter. The basic problem of financing is how to raise the necessary resources so as to meet the cost when it has to be paid. There are, however, different aspects to this problem. One is that the resources must be raised in a regular and systematic way, even though the benefits fall due at irregular intervals, in the short term and in the long term. There is also the question of how the resources should be raised — whether from taxation or from contributions levied on the covered persons and, where employed persons are concerned, on the employers.

With certain types of scheme, the solution to the financing problem is obvious. Universal schemes covering all residents and social assistance schemes are naturally financed out of taxation, with resources being raised so as to cover costs. Occupational schemes restricted to specific groups of employees must be financed out of contributions, with resources being raised in advance of costs so as to provide a measure of security for the employees in respect of benefits which have been earned. Provident funds are, of course, financed out of contributions, with individual members benefiting from the accumulated total of contributions made by them or on their behalf by employers. With social insurance schemes, however, a variety of methods are possible and each can be justified on different grounds. What follows is therefore mainly concerned with social insurance schemes.

FACTORS AFFECTING THE COST AND ITS TREND

Similar benefits in different countries will not necessarily cost the same in relation to the respective level of wages. Inherent characteristics, such as the age and sex distribution and differing economic activity of the population, will affect the incidence, the frequency and the duration of claims; and attitudes towards claiming benefit may vary. The nature of the working environment will condition certain risks. The relative strictness or laxity with which the scheme is administered will be reflected in the cost both of administration and of benefits.

Short-term benefits

Short-term benefits are payable after a relatively short qualifying period, if any, and for limited periods of time, generally for one year or less. They include sickness and maternity cash benefits, medical care benefit, and benefit in respect of temporary incapacity following employment injury. Family benefits and unemployment benefit are also included in this category.

The vital statistics which underlie claims for maternity and family benefits are highly regular in their incidence, changing only slowly over the years. Similarly, sickness and death recur with a natural regularity, though this may be temporarily disturbed by epidemics. The incidence of employment injury varies greatly between occupations but, if the distribution of occupations is relatively stable, the total cost to the benefit scheme will not fluctuate much. On the other hand, unemployment, unlike the "biological" contingencies, is not characterised by a statistical regularity; its incidence may vary widely, unpredictably and at short notice.

A qualifying period is usual in all branches of social insurance schemes except employment injury, and it is sometimes a feature in the organisation of medical care and family benefits; this keeps down the number of successful claims, at least to begin with. So, normally, a person who is sick or unemployed when contributions start to be collected will not be awarded benefit for that spell of absence from work. The effect of the qualifying period varies, of course, with its length; once a scheme has been in force for the length of the qualifying period, persons who have entered the scheme in the meantime will progressively satisfy the condition for the relevant benefit. That is the point at which the cost of short-term benefit (as a percentage of the insured wage bill of the active population) will rise steadily over a short period. It will then remain at a fairly stable level. Although it may vary slightly up and down, these variations will not be very wide or long-lasting except in the case of unemployment benefit.

The cost of benefits will naturally depend upon the number of claims awarded, the average rate of benefit, the waiting period, if any, and the maximum period for which benefit may be payable. A waiting period excludes minor cases of short duration. The maximum benefit period eliminates the chronic cases which, though few in number, might continue indefinitely. Chronic cases are thereafter handled under other arrangements: continuing sickness is usually treated as invalidity; continuing incapacity following an industrial accident as disablement; and chronic unemployment may be taken over and financed by an unemployment assistance scheme. Limits of cost or duration may be placed upon medical care benefit, and the cost of family benefit may be contained by setting limits to the age or number of eligible children within the family group.

The readiness of the covered population to take advantage of the scheme affects the cost, particularly in the sickness and medical care branches. As a rule, protected persons may visit a doctor as often as they wish and the doctor will, in most cases, prescribe some form of medicine. So the cost of medical care will substantially reflect the attitude which persons in the community customarily take towards their state of health. The progress of medicine has not, in general, led to a fall in the frequency of illness. Today people are apparently more aware of, and more concerned about, their state of health than their fathers were. The soaring cost of medical care is accounted for not only by the rise in unit cost of the services but also by the increasing use made of them.

The influence of the working environment is most evident in the employment injury branch. The frequency and severity of injuries vary from country to country, depending not only on the kind of industries, and the extent to which they use dangerous material, processes and machinery, but also on the local attitude towards safety precautions, on the quality of medical care, and on the strictness of industrial and medical supervision.

The unemployment benefit branch, when placed under pressure of mounting claims and labour turnover, presents a picture of its own. If unemployment rises above a certain level, the volume of claims may actually decline, because the number of persons who have exhausted their benefit rights increases more rapidly than the number of fresh claimants. When unemployment is widespread, in a period of recession the concentration of demand for benefit in certain sectors may mean that many insured persons in these sectors exhaust their right to benefit and their protection for the time being. In more favoured sectors, on the other hand, many covered persons remain in steady employment. An unemployment insurance scheme is almost invariably designed to provide a short-term benefit. The risk is pooled widely but for a limited period and the transfer of chronic cases to assistance arrangements ensures that the scheme remains solvent.

Long-term benefits

Long-term benefits include old-age, invalidity and survivors' benefits, together with the benefits for disablement and for dependants payable under employment injury insurance.

As with short-term benefits, the qualifying period delays the initial build-up of the number of old-age pensioners in a newly established scheme; however, this is counterbalanced to some extent by transitional provisions which shorten the qualifying period for persons already elderly when the scheme is put into force. After the minimum qualifying period has elapsed, the number of pensioners continues to grow for many years and, for this and for other reasons, the annual cost of the scheme in relation to the insured wage bill continues to grow for an even longer period. So the trend in the cost of long-term benefits differs from that of short-term benefits, which reaches reasonable stability comparatively soon.

Every year yields its new crop of pensioners, the majority of whom (orphans excepted) are likely to draw a pension for the rest of their lives. If we look at the characteristics of the largest group of these — old-age pensioners — we see that a fresh "cohort" is added to the total every year and that some members of each age cohort will die each year, the last one doing so after a period which may be as great as 20 or even 30 years. The following figures have been deliberately simplified for illustration but give some indication of the process. If there are 100 pensioners in the first year, there may be (say) 196 in the second, 288 in the third, 800 in the tenth, and 1,000 in the twentieth. From this rough illustration it can be seen that the number almost doubles annually at the start and thereafter increases relatively more slowly to reach, after some 20 years, a figure of ten times the initial figure.

If a larger number of young people enter employment, the proportion of pensioners in the whole insured population will grow more slowly. Conversely, a reduction in the number of young recruits will accelerate the rise in the proportion of pensioners. This is an aspect of the ageing of the population which is causing concern in some developed countries.

The effect of the benefit rate or formula on the volume of benefit expenditure must also be considered. Unless all pensioners enjoy the same standard rate of pension, the cost of the benefits will continue to grow long after the number of pensioners has reached a stable level. The reason for this is that, as the rate of pension is generally proportional to the length of the contribution record, the average rate of new pensions awarded each year will rise in comparison with the rate of those which terminate. Furthermore, where the rate of pension is related to the wage at or near retirement, wage inflation will cause new pensions to be even higher than those awarded previously. In addition, existing pensions may also be revised periodically in order to compensate for the effects of inflation.

Normal pensionable age

Although, in general, the cost of old-age pensions is increasing, there are also certain key factors which affect the cost of old-age pension schemes. One such factor is normal pensionable age, the raising or lowering of which has a surprisingly significant effect. If the age is raised, there will be fewer old-age pensions, but at the same time the number of contributors will be larger; this effect will, however, be partly offset by an increase in the number of invalidity pensioners and in expenditure on invalidity pensions. The lowering of the pensionable age will produce converse effects.

Rates of mortality at the normal pensionable age and at higher ages must also be considered. Life expectancy at birth is often used as an indicator of the overall mortality conditions in a country or region, but it is not directly relevant to the fixing of the pensionable age. It would be misleading to argue that, because the life expectancy at birth is much lower in a developing country than in an industrialised country, the pensionable age in the former should be fixed at a correspondingly lower level. Life expectancy at birth is affected to a considerable extent by the infant mortality rate, which is high in developing countries. As those who survive their first few years in developing countries grow older, their life expectancy levels approach closer to those prevailing in the industrialised countries. Table 6 shows that the difference in life expectancy at the age of 60 or 65 is much less significant than at earlier ages.

Long-standing universal pension schemes in industrialised countries have already been through their initial period of growth and have attained a certain maturity. Nevertheless, even in these countries, the increasing cost of pensions is causing concern. This phenomenon is partly due to the ageing of the population. In most industrialised countries the ratio of old people to those of working age has been growing for the past half-century or more and the process is expected to continue for some decades at least. It is true that simultaneously the proportion of children in most of these countries has tended to decline. But the problem remains because an old-age pensioner costs several times as much as a child to maintain. Table 7 presents some census figures and United Nations forecasts illustrating these trends.

The increasing cost of pensions follows not only from demographic trends but also from the regular raising of benefit rates in response to social demands; the regular and often automatic adjustment of pensions to preserve their purchasing power; and, in periods of recession, the encouragement given to older workers, who might otherwise have continued in work, to retire. Hence, serious consideration is now being given in various quarters to the best strategy for effectively raising the pensionable age — a difficult problem which has also been touched on in other chapters.

Table 6.   Comparative expectation of life of males in selected countries at various reference years between 1960 and 1980 (in years)

Country and year(s) of reference	Expectation of life at: Birth	Age 20	Age 60	Age 65
Brazil 1960-70	57.6	47.0	15.0	12.0
Chile 1975-80	61.3	48.4	15.9	12.8
France 1978-80	70.1	51.6	17.1	13.8
Fed. Rep. of Germany 1978-80	69.6	51.4	16.3	12.9
Islamic Republic of Iran 1973-76	57.6	49.7	16.1	13.0
Kenya 1969	49.9	43.0	14.5	11.7
Liberia 1971	45.8	40.8	14.9	12.3
Syrian Arab Republic 1977	63.0	50.8	16.0	12.8

Source. United Nations: *Demographic Yearbook 1978* (New York, 1979); idem: *Demographic Yearbook 1981* (New York, 1983).

Table 7.   Changing profile of populations, by broad age groups, in Europe and North America (distribution per 1,000 of population)

Age groups	Europe		North America	
	1975	2000 [1]	1975	2000 [1]
Under 15 years	239	206	252	217
15 to 64 years	638	651	645	662
65 years and over	123	143	103	121

[1] The figures in the column are estimates only.
Source. United Nations: *Concise report on the world population situation in 1979* (New York, doc. ST/ESA/SER.A72, 1980).

METHODICAL RAISING OF RESOURCES

As mentioned earlier, one important aspect of the financing of social insurance schemes is how to plan and manage the raising of resources systematically, so as to meet the cost of benefits and the cost of administration as and when they arise.

Annual assessment system

In the case of short-term benefits, because the annual cost attains a stable level in relation to the insured wage bill in a relatively short time, the financing method which suggests itself is the "assessment" or "pay-as-you-go" system, under which resources raised year by year exactly balance the expected cost year by year. Applied in this way, it is termed the "annual assessment system". A small margin is usually allowed in order to build up a "contingency reserve", the purpose of which is to help meet an unforeseen rise in expenditure or fall in income due to accidental fluctuations in the system. It is impossible to tell in advance of actual experience what the level of the reserve should be but, while a sickness insurance scheme can be comfortable with a few months' contributions in reserve, an unemployment fund could not be secure without a much larger amount to fall back on. The initial period during which qualifying conditions are being satisfied facilitates the building up of the reserve.

In the case of long-term benefits, more complex considerations come into play. At the beginning of a new contributory pension scheme, the cost of benefits is comparatively modest for some years (even if special concessions are made to enable elderly new entrants to the scheme to qualify for pension earlier than the standard rules might allow). To cover this cost under the annual assessment system, year by year, could have unfortunate consequences. The impression might be created that a quite generous pension scheme could be financed by a modest rate of contribution. In due course, as increasing numbers of the insured population qualified for pension, the total annual cost would rise steeply and the annual assessment required to meet that cost would also rise as steeply — to the point where it would not be possible to find the cost from the wages of current contributors. A major reconstruction of the finances of the scheme might then be needed.

Some method of funding future liabilities for contributory pensions must be adopted which recognises that such liabilities are being created from the beginning of the scheme and that a prudent level of reserves must be built up to meet them as they emerge with the ageing of the population. In practice, a few systems have been identified as particularly appropriate for social insurance. Even amongst these systems, however, a number of considerations have to be taken into account if the most appropriate system is to be chosen for a particular country.

There are, broadly speaking, two methods of financing pension insurance so as to secure an equilibrium between an income which is constant or slowly rising and an expenditure which is rising rapidly. The first method is to cover the whole future cost of each year's crop of pensions in the year of their award. The second method, which admits of several variants, relies on the accumulation of capital, the investment of which will provide additional income in the future.

Assessment of constituent capitals system

The first method is called the "assessment of constituent capitals system" and consists in equating each year's income to the capital value of the pensions awarded in that year. Thus, supposing, for example, that the capital value of a pension is ten times its annual amount, the contribution needed in a given year will be ten times the sum of the annual amounts of the pensions awarded in that year. Apart from financing any increase in the number of new pensions awarded each year, the resources required will rise only if there is an increase in the average amount of the pensions awarded. However, such an increase in the charge is likely to be acceptable since it may well be that a corresponding increase in the income per head of the population concerned will more than keep pace with it.

This method in its simplest form seems never to have been used for any general scheme of pension insurance. In employment injury insurance, on the other hand, it has been and still is the typical technique for covering pension liabilities arising from permanent disablement or death. Here the rate of the pension is not affected by the length of the individual's participation in the scheme. If the number of accidents giving rise to such awards remained constant from year to year, so probably would the total amount of resources required when expressed, for example, as a percentage of the whole contributory wage bill; this percentage might, however, fluctuate for individual employers if the employment injury benefit costs were spread among employers in proportion to their record of accidents (the so-called "merit rating" system).

Systems of capital accumulation

So far as pension insurance (old-age, survivors' and invalidity insurance) is concerned, a second method — namely, that which accumulates capital, not to be expended but for the sake of the interest it yields — has been widely favoured. It makes use of the fact that a compulsory social insurance scheme is sure of recruiting every year a supply of young contributors to replace the annual crop of pensioners. Since such a scheme will never be liquidated, it need not accumulate — as must an occupational pension scheme — the capital value of the benefit rights which the insured persons, as individuals, have acquired and are in the process of acquiring. In practice, therefore, the scheme has only to arrange that the current resources plus interest on reserves will cover current expenditure at all times.

One of the advantages of this method is that it offers a solution to the problem of financing the concessions that are usually granted to the older members of the initially insured population, securing to them a minimum pension, not balanced by their contributions, after only a short qualifying period. It would be unfair to charge the cost of these privileges only to the younger members of the initial population. The method described distributes the charge not only over that population but also over the unlimited series of its successors.

General average premium

Within this general approach there are a number of possible variants. One extreme possibility is to determine at the outset a constant rate of resources, as a percentage of the insured wage bill, which, on the assumptions made, can ensure the financial viability of the scheme *ad infinitum*. This financing system is called the "general average premium" system. The accumulation of capital under the general average premium system would nevertheless be sizeable and in many developing countries it could be an embarrassment to the authority responsible for investment policies.

The institutions of pension insurance are often required to invest in bonds guaranteed by the State, that is, in securities yielding a fixed interest. A considerable portion of the capital of many social insurance institutions has been used in this way to finance programmes of public housing and other public building work. A real addition has thereby been made to the national wealth, whether ultimately profitable to the institution or not. Too often, however, these large accumulations of capital have been misused and dissipated, for they offer extraordinary temptations.

In the developed countries the extension of pension insurance to embrace the great majority of the economically active population has caused the policy of accumulating capital to appear in a somewhat new perspective. When such schemes were of moderate size, it was reasonable to plan for their future solvency to be buttressed by the investment of funds with the nation as a whole. But when the scope of the insurance scheme became practically co-extensive with the nation's taxpayers, the contributors appeared to be lending to themselves and being taxed to pay the interest on the loan. Also, since there was no assurance that the loan would be used to improve the nation's productivity, the money might perhaps have been more profitably employed if it had remained at the disposal of its producers.

These, it seems, were the considerations that prompted the United Kingdom to decide, as long ago as 1925, to introduce a general scheme of pension insurance that operates without accumulating any large permanent capital, the annually increasing deficit being covered by taxation. Similar policies have been followed by certain countries which have seen the capital of their general schemes reduced to insignificance by the inflation that accompanied and followed the Second World War.

Nevertheless, it should not be concluded that the method of accumulating capital has been, or ought to be, abandoned. This method will still be desirable and expedient where pensions are provided through insurance schemes that cover only a relatively small part of the population or where state subsidies are difficult to provide. Such a situation is now found in most developing countries. Here capital accumulation is an evident choice, not only for technical reasons related to the insurance fund but also because it is highly beneficial to the national economy. Moreover, some developed countries with schemes of broad scope nevertheless emphasise the need for a certain accumulation of funds either to compensate for reduced national savings resulting from a decrease of savings under private pension schemes or as a part of an anti-inflationary policy.

Scaled premium system

The so-called "scaled premium system", which is an intermediate approach between the general average premium system and the assessment system, has much to commend it. Under this system, the rate at which current resources are raised is fixed at a certain percentage of the insured wage bill so that there should be a balance between receipts and expenditure over a certain "period of equilibrium" such as ten or 15 years. When current resources (including contribution income and interest from investments) are no longer sufficient to cover costs, the percentage rate is raised to a level sufficient for another equilibrium period. This system does not as a rule provide for the use of the principal of the accumulated fund but only for the use of the interest which it generates. Thus, it is possible to place the accumulated fund in long-term investments. The accumulation of capital under this scaled premium approach is comparatively small and it can be regulated in advance by selecting a more or less lengthy "period of equilibrium". Also this system is flexible in that it gives the responsible finance authorities the possibility of gradually adapting the raising of resources for the social security programme to the development of the economy.

Another factor in financial management is the adjustment of pensions for changes in the purchasing power of the currency due to inflation. In any funded financial system, such adjustments require that the value of the accumulated reserves should appreciate correspondingly, unless funds are made available from other sources. However, it is difficult to place huge reserves in investments which maintain their real value; and the larger the reserves the more acute the problem becomes. Thus, paradoxical as it may seem, adjustments of pensions are relatively easier under the scaled premium system with its lower ratio of funding than under the general average premium system.

DISTRIBUTION AMONG POPULATION SECTORS

Having determined the financial system for a social insurance scheme, it is necessary to decide how these resources will be shared among the various population sectors. The main distinction here is between financing through contributions — that is, payments by covered persons and their employers — and financing through taxation — general revenue financing, special taxes specifically allocated, value-added tax, and so on. There are the further questions of how the contributions should be shared between employers and employees; whether the contributions should be flat-rate or earnings-related; and how the contribution rates should be varied according to the level of wages — including the adoption of a wage ceiling for contribution purposes.

Tripartite financing

It will be recalled that Bismarck's social insurance programme was made possible by the device of the joint contribution of the insured person (in this case the employee) and the employer, supplemented by a state subsidy. This arrangement has been adopted in many countries as the mechanism for financing the social insurance system. Certain arguments which have become traditional are invoked in order to justify recourse to each of the three participants.

The insured person's contribution represents part of the sum that the person could be expected to save or pay to a mutual benefit society or insurance company for somewhat comparable protection against the risk or risks in question. Its psychological import is considerable. It sustains the sense of responsibility of the contributor and the dignity of the beneficiary. And it supplies the visible evidence of the insured person's right to benefit and perhaps to having a voice in the management of the scheme.

Employers also derive advantages from social insurance. In industrialised countries and in developing countries alike, social insurance helps to maintain industrial peace and the stability of the social order. Its medical benefits also conserve the employees' productive capacity. Thus, industry would be less prosperous without social insurance.

The community at large is interested in the general health and welfare of the workforce. Any citizens with a social conscience will understand the moral and material value of social security and will be willing according to their ability to support what is in effect a mutual benefit society on a national scale.

It is instructive to view the contributions of employees and employers as alternative and complementary resources. The remuneration of employees must suffice to cover their needs, not only while they are earning, but also while they are unable to earn. Social insurance is the mechanism by which their remuneration is distributed between these two alternative situations.

If employees are indeed enjoying a fair share of what they produce, they are already receiving their entire remuneration, and so there is no surplus at the employer's disposal from which to pay a contribution. It might be concluded from this that employees should pay the whole cost of their protection. Starting when they are young and healthy, they will be able to spare from their earnings the premiums required to insure the payment of benefits that are substantial in relation to their wages in sickness and old age. But social insurance is compulsory, embracing good and bad risks together and particularly the old as well as the young. Are the good risks to take upon themselves the additional premium that the bad risks demand? Surely this is a charge to be distributed in the name of social solidarity as widely as possible according to taxable capacity. Employers are generally in a better position than workers to bear the impact of this additional premium.

However, the assumption that the employees are receiving their fair and entire remuneration is a notional one that is made for the sake of argument; what that remuneration may be is a matter of opinion, not of fact.

In imposing a contribution, whether on employees or on employers, it is the initial step itself which is most difficult. The saying that an old tax is no tax is relevant here. Once the contribution has been introduced, the contributors will find ways of adapting themselves to it.

It may be concluded that each source of revenue has advantages and disadvantages. The ultimate costs cannot as a rule be determined and prudence suggests that misjudgements and shock will be minimised if, in the social security system as a whole, each of the sources is drawn upon in moderation.

The Social Security (Minimum Standards) Convention, 1952 (No. 102), lays down the following principles for member States:

> The cost of the benefits provided in compliance with this Convention and the cost of the administration of such benefits shall be borne collectively by way of insurance contributions or taxation or both in a manner which avoids hardship to persons of small means and takes into account the economic situation of the Member and of the classes of persons protected.

The Convention sets a maximum limit for the contribution of employees as a class:

> The total of the insurance contributions borne by the employees protected shall not exceed 50 per cent of the total of the financial resources allocated to the protection of employees and their wives and children. For the purpose of ascertaining whether this condition is fulfilled, all the benefits provided by the Member in compliance with this Convention, except family benefit and, if provided by a special branch, employment injury benefit, may be taken together.

It will be noted that the Convention, while safeguarding the worker from being saddled with more than one-half of any social insurance contribution, does not lay down any formal requirement about how the costs should otherwise be shared, beyond that hardship should be avoided to persons of small means and that the economic situation of the State and of covered persons should be taken into account.

Financing by the State and by employers

In the USSR, and in some of the other countries of Eastern Europe, the employee pays no contribution. The entire cost of the social security system is borne by the employers and the State, at least so far as the workers in state-owned undertakings are concerned.

Elsewhere the State may subsidise the social security system. A state subsidy may take different forms: for instance, a fixed proportion of each pension awarded, an allocation proportional to the contributions paid by employers and employees, a fixed annual subvention, or simply what is needed to cover any deficit that occurs. The subsidy may also take an indirect form, as when sickness insurance schemes avail themselves of public hospitals and pay much less than the actual cost of the care given to their patients. The State may assume all or the greater part of the charge for certain benefits which are considered particularly conducive to social welfare, such as family allowances or a national health service.

Family allowances are provided either under a universal scheme financed by taxation or under an insurance scheme to which the employers are, in almost all cases, the sole contributors.

The cost of employment injury is borne, in most countries, by the employers alone. The United Kingdom is one of the few countries which finance the cash benefits of employment injury insurance on a tripartite basis. There are several countries, however, that charge the cost of the temporary incapacity and medical benefits wholly or partly to sickness insurance. In certain countries employers pay employment injury insurance premiums calculated according to the average risk of the class to which their undertakings belong (the differential rating system). Some schemes even provide for an upward or downward adjustment of the premium based on the individual accident record of the establishment (the merit rating system); it is sometimes believed that this procedure encourages safety measures. Nevertheless, other schemes have their employment injury insurance financed on a uniform scale by all establishments. Where the risk of employment injury is covered under a workmen's compensation scheme based on the concept of employers' liability, with commercial insurance, the premiums are invariably fixed on differential and merit rating principles.

Statistical comparison

A brief analysis of the income of selected social security systems, according to sources, is given in table 8. The figures are derived from statistics collected by the ILO in the course of its continuous study of the cost of social security systems. They include the income not only of social insurance and family allowance schemes but also of public health services, public assistance schemes and benefit schemes for public servants and for war victims. Although data have been extracted for only 19 countries, these are sufficient to show how widely different are the financial policies followed and how unimportant the income from accumulated capital has now become in certain countries. It seems quite clear that financial policies are governed much more by considerations of practicability than by any abstract principles.

METHODS OF FIXING CONTRIBUTIONS

Contributions payable by insured persons and by employers may be flat-rate, that is, uniform for all insured persons, or earnings-related (the term "wage-related" is interchangeable).

Where flat-rate contributions are the rule, benefits are usually payable at flat rates. The system is easy to understand and to administer. However, it is strongly regressive, since, as a proportion of earnings, the contribution bears more heavily upon lower-paid workers than upon others. The system may be appropriate in schemes which aim to provide a certain minimum level of benefit, but it is not appropriate where earnings-related benefits are to be provided. Nevertheless, flat-rate contributions are sometimes found in earnings-related insurance schemes when they have been extended to admit self-employed or non-employed persons, perhaps on a voluntary basis, and to allow them to qualify for flat-rate benefits.

As regards earnings-related contributions, they may be fixed as a straight percentage of actual earnings or on the basis of earnings classes for each of which a specific flat-rate contribution applies. In either case, it is the usual practice not to take earnings above a prescribed upper limit into account for determining contributions or benefits. That limit should obviously not be too low. It must define a range of wages within which earnings-related benefit has a real meaning for the majority of workers. (On occasion, pressure is exercised not to set the limit too high, but to leave an area within which private pension plans may operate "on top of the state scheme".) Earnings-related contributions may be adjudged more equitable than flat-rate contributions and be applied with a progressive series of percentages so as to levy a smaller contribution from lower wage earners than from those at the upper end of the scale. It is sometimes

Table 8. Receipts of social security systems of selected countries in 1977 distributed according to origin and expressed as percentages of gross domestic product

Country	Distribution of social security receipts according to origin (per 100 of total receipts)							Total receipts as percentages of gross domestic product
	Contributions		Special taxes allocated to social security	State participation	Participation of other public authorities	Income from capital	Other receipts	
	Insured persons	Employers						
Belgium	18.1	41.7	0.2	33.8	1.3	2.2	2.7	25.6
Chile	17.5	45.6	1.0	29.7	–	2.5	3.7	13.2
Czechoslovakia	0.0	2.6	–	95.8	–	–	1.6	19.0
Denmark	1.4	5.5	–	58.4	33.0	1.7	0.0	24.5
France	19.4	55.7	1.9	19.7	1.6	1.0	0.7	26.0
Federal Republic of Germany	29.5	41.1	0.4	26.0	–	1.3	1.7	23.0
Guatemala	26.1	41.1	–	31.7	–	–	1.1	2.1
India [1]	66.1 [3]		0.5	2.8	19.5	10.9	0.2	4.2
Italy	13.5	61.2	–	16.5	4.7	2.4	1.7	20.8
Japan [2]	25.0	28.8	–	27.9	3.9	8.2	6.2	12.5
Kenya	19.6	26.5	0.0	38.1	–	14.9	0.9	2.9
Netherlands	35.7	38.2	–	16.6	1.4	7.6	0.5	31.4
New Zealand [2]	3.1	5.4	0.0	89.6	–	1.9	–	18.8
Poland	1.2	57.4	–	30.1	11.0	0.2	0.1	12.9
Senegal [1]	8.7	44.1	–	46.2	–	0.1	0.9	2.8
Sweden	1.2	44.1	–	20.6	26.7	7.4	–	33.9
USSR	–	–	–	96.4	–	–	3.6	13.4
United Kingdom [2]	17.7	29.5	–	43.4	7.1	2.2	0.1	18.8
United States [2]	21.4	35.6	–	26.4	11.4	5.2	–	14.8

– Not applicable.   0.0 Magnitude less than half the unit used.
[1] Year 1975-76.   [2] Year 1976-77.   [3] The figure relates to the sum of insured persons' and employers' contributions. A breakdown is not available.

Source: ILO: The Cost of Social Security: Tenth International Inquiry, 1975-1977 (Geneva, 1981).

argued that upper limits to contributions conflict with the general principle of solidarity which underlies social security. When such limits exist, they are revised in line with the movement of economic indicators and may be abolished altogether.

INVESTMENT OF RESERVE FUNDS

Funds which are accumulated under the pay-as-you-go system of finance, that is, reserves which are established to meet unexpected emergencies, should be invested in short-term investments with a high degree of liquidity. Other reserves, which arise from current resources in excess of current disbursements under the scaled premium, general average premium and assessment of constituent capitals systems of finance, may be invested in long-term investments.

The basic principles which govern the investment of social security funds are not different from those of other fiduciary organisations: safety, yield and liquidity. However, another factor should be considered after the first three prerequisites have been met: social and economic utility.

The safety of the investment depends not only on the preservation of the capital invested, in nominal terms, but also on the maintenance of the real value of the investment. This implies that capital appreciation should be sought in an investment. Maintenance of the real value of investments is particularly important during periods of inflation, as it facilitates the adjustment that must be made to pensions in order to compensate them for the loss of purchasing power which results from increases in the cost of living.

The yield on investments is of particular importance in the case of the reserve funds which support long-term benefits. The net yield rate on these investments must at least be equal to the rate of interest assumed for the actuarial estimates. Otherwise, it may be necessary to raise additional resources over and above those foreseen by the actuary. In any financial system which operates on the basis of advance funding (either full or partial) of the benefits, a satisfactory yield on the invested assets is necessary in order that the current resources required should remain within reasonable limits.

The liquidity of the investment is directly related to the cash flow projections of the income and expenditure of the scheme. Any investment of contingency reserves in respect of short-term benefits must be readily realisable. On the other hand, the investments made in respect of the reserve funds for long-term benefits financed under the scaled premium, general average premium or assessment of constituent capitals systems need not be readily realisable and may be placed in long-term securities. The investments of a provident fund are also normally of a long-term nature; however, care must be taken in projecting the future cash flows of a provident fund since at the time a benefit is payable the entire credit of a member, rather than just a (smaller) periodic amount, is paid out.

Finally, when safety, yield and liquidity have been taken into consideration, social security funds should, to the extent possible, be invested in order to improve the overall quality of life in the country. Investments in the health and education infrastructure and in enterprises which create employment opportunities are in this category. One important principle, however, is that the funds should be invested only through financial intermediaries, so that the attention of the management of the social security scheme is not diverted from its primary concern of ensuring the efficient operation of the scheme.

ACTUARIAL VALUATIONS

Social insurance schemes (especially those providing pensions) which have been established without actuarial preparation or with deliberate disregard of actuarial requirements have, in the long run, disappointed the expectations of their beneficiaries. Even a scheme established on a sound actuarial basis may be rendered ineffective by unforeseen changes. For this reason Convention No. 102 requires governments to evaluate the assets and liabilities of social security schemes periodically, in order to ensure that the schemes maintain their solvency, and to fix rates of benefit and contributions on the basis of actuarial estimates.

An actuary recommends both the initial rates of contribution required for the various benefits and the appropriate financial organisation. Before making any recommendations, however, the actuary must collect and analyse economic and demographic data which have a bearing on the operation of the social security scheme. If, as is frequently the case, these data are unavailable, incomplete or unreliable, the recommendations must be made on the basis of assumptions which in the actuary's best judgement are appropriate to the scheme.

In formulating recommendations for short-term benefits, the actuary must know the following factors for each individual contingency (or component of a contingency — for example, medical care is subdivided into consultations, visits, medicaments, hospitalisation, etc.):

(a) the frequency of occurrence of the contingency or component;

(b) the number of units of benefit per case; and

(c) the average cost per benefit unit.

In formulating recommendations for long-term benefits, data or assumptions on a substantial number of elements are required. Some of the factors which the actuary must consider are: the total insured population and the age and sex distribution of the insured population; the annual rate of increase in the insured population; the mortality rates of the insured population and of persons receiving old-age, invalidity and survivors' pensions; the proportion of male insured persons who are married; the distribution of ages of wives at various ages of husbands; the number of children and their age distribution at various ages of insured workers; the density of employment (the proportion of a period worked by insured persons); the average insured earnings and the progression of average insured earnings by age; the expected increases in insured earnings in the future; the rate of interest which may be earned for various durations of investments to be made in the future; and the expenses of administration.

In making the initial financial recommendations, it would be impossible for an actuary to select a set of assumptions and later find that they had all been realised in practice. Rather, the actuary must draw on experience and on the data available in order to recommend a system which will permit the scheme to commence operations on a sound basis. Subsequent actuarial valuations, in the light of the statistical and financial data gathered while the scheme is in operation, will result in the refinement of the original assumptions and the recommendation of modifications in the contribution rates and in other aspects of the scheme. Such actuarial valuations, which are intended to ensure that the scheme continues to operate on a sound financial basis, are generally statutory requirements, to be undertaken every three or five years.

SOCIAL SECURITY AND THE NATIONAL ECONOMY 13

A PERSONAL SERVICE AND ITS REPERCUSSIONS

A social security benefit scheme is essentially a personal service to covered persons and their dependants, and its success is measured primarily in those terms. But the foundation and strength of a scheme lie in its being rooted in the national economy and its secondary effects can be seen in the economy generally. One familiar effect was enlarged upon in a report [1] prepared by the ILO for a developing country, as follows:

Modern social security programmes may be regarded as devices to redistribute income within their field and, according to their structure, may divert part of the fruits of current production for the benefit of injured workers; secure minimum pensions for lower-paid workers, partly at the expense of their better-paid colleagues; spread the social cost of widowhood, invalidity, etc., more widely by appropriate tax measures; be the means by which the industrial sector can directly assist the development of basic health services for the country at large — and in general go some way towards redressing the economic balance in favour of the relatively underprivileged.

This chapter will deal briefly with the ways in which social security interacts with economic and social development, and its repercussions on consumption and production, wages and employment, savings and investment.

SOCIAL SECURITY AND ECONOMIC DEVELOPMENT

Economic development is characterised by the progressive use of cash in the economy, the growth and increasing mechanisation of factory industries and a change in population balance from country to town. As the process goes on, structural changes take place in the organisation and means of living. Workers hitherto accustomed to rural subsistence within their village or tribal family find themselves in an urban setting totally dependent on money wages. In the changed economic setting, social security programmes become imperative to protect workers against the risks which menace their regular incomes and their ability to support themselves and their families. In other words, social security becomes a crucial element in industrialisation, economic development and growth.

The pattern and "mix" of a social security programme will clearly depend upon the order of priority in which a number of variables are placed. Such variables include the structure of economic and industrial programmes and the perceived needs of the workforce in the individual country, the established pattern of social and family life and likely developments in this regard, the degree of dissociation between workers and their home village life, the customary age of retirement or earlier withdrawal from urban employment, the importance of medical services as against cash sickness benefit, and so on. The decision to start or to develop particular benefits in a particular sector will be made with the planned longer-term programme in mind.

Table 9 sets out the receipts, total expenditure and cost of benefits in a selection of countries, as a percentage of their gross domestic product, for two financial years a few years apart and in this way compares and contrasts the growth of national systems in financial terms.

There are a number of unknown and variable factors in this 13-country table. It is not shown, for example, how inflation affected the real value of benefits or, indeed, the scope and coverage of benefits in each country. Three general inferences may fairly be made:

1. In every instance quoted, over the years shown, the country has devoted an increased amount of its gross domestic product to social security. Unless it is to be assumed that programmes have a natural momentum of their own, it may fairly be concluded that social security is growing in response to a real need and appreciation of its value in the economy.

2. Where social security programmes have been in operation for several generations, they constitute a most important sector of the national economy, disposing of anything from one-sixth to one-quarter of the gross domestic product of the countries included in the table.

3. From a broad comparison between receipts and expenditure, it appears that the developing countries listed may, on the whole, be building up reserves, presumably because they are operating funded pension schemes or provident funds for old age; while, in the case of the fully developed programmes, either a sufficient total volume of reserves has been built up over the years or the economies of the respective countries have reached a stage of development and maturity which enables them to sustain their social security expenditure without embarrassment on a year-to-year basis.

The content of the social security programme is bound to influence and mould the direction and rate of economic development to a significant degree.

Medical care schemes organised within the framework of social

Table 9. Receipts, expenditure and benefits under social security schemes expressed as a percentage of gross domestic product at purchaser's value

Country	Financial year	Receipts	Expenditure	
			Total	Benefits
Africa				
Ethiopia	1971-72 [1]	1.7	1.3	1.3
	1975-76 [1]	2.5	1.8	1.8
Tunisia	1965 [1]	3.4	3.1	2.6
	1977 [1]	5.6	3.2	2.8
Zambia	1965 [1]	2.1	1.9	1.9
	1976-77	6.2	4.6	4.4
America				
Brazil	1965 [1]	4.5	4.3	3.4
	1977 [1]	6.2	6.2	5.3
Jamaica	1964-65 [1]	2.9	2.7	2.5
	1976-77	5.9	4.4	3.9
Panama	1960 [1]	7.7	6.3	6.0
	1977 [1]	9.9	7.9	7.0
Asia				
Burma	1964-65 [1]	1.0	0.9	0.9
	1976-77 [1]	1.2	1.2	1.2
India	1959-60 [1]	1.9	1.4	1.4
	1975-76	4.2	2.4	2.4
Japan	1964-65	6.6	5.1	4.6
	1976-77	12.5	9.7	8.6
Europe				
Belgium	1960 [1]	15.5	15.3	13.7
	1977 [1]	25.6	25.5	23.7
Federal Republic of Germany	1960	16.3	15.4	14.6
	1977	23.0	23.4	22.4
Czechoslovakia [2]	1960	15.4	15.4	15.3
	1977	19.0	19.0	18.9
Oceania				
New Zealand	1964-65	12.0	11.5	10.9
	1976-77	18.8	18.2	18.1

[1] As a percentage of the gross domestic product computed in accordance with the old System of Normal Accounts (SNA) prior to the adoption by the United Nations in 1968 of a new SNA. [2] As a percentage of net material product.
Source. ILO: *The Cost of Social Security: Tenth International Inquiry, 1975-1977* (Geneva, 1981).

security help to promote a fit and efficient workforce and have a direct effect on productivity and economic growth. In earlier chapters it has been pointed out how the social security administration may contribute to general medical care and to preventive measures which are organised within the framework of public health services. Family benefits and medical care promote the health both of scholars and trainees and of the active workforce, and the national community will benefit from the fitness and productivity not only of those already in the labour force but also of those who are equipping themselves in their formative years.

The availability of cash benefits is also important. The replacement of wages during illness or unemployment, after injury at work, or when a woman is confined, guards against a drop in the standard of living. Moreover, the assurance that this will be so removes one of the oldest traditional anxieties which has menaced the manual worker and professional alike. Taken together, these considerations promote stability of manpower and reduce absenteeism. They should also facilitate mobility of labour because benefit rights under social security are not dependent on continuing employment with one employer.

It is occasionally alleged that some benefits, especially unemployment and sickness benefits, may be set at a level which encourages absenteeism and malingering. At the planning stage, and during administration of the scheme, careful attention to the qualifying conditions for benefit and the methods of control of beneficiaries could be expected to curb or mitigate such adverse effects.

By themselves, or more often in collaboration with the authorities responsible for occupational safety and health, many social security administrations undertake specific measures against the risks of employment accident and occupational disease. Once again, although the motive is primarily the personal protection of employed persons, the broader economic effect of such measures cannot be overlooked.

The substantial surpluses which are generated by social insurance schemes for long-term benefits and by provident funds make important contributions to economic growth in many developing countries.

SOCIAL SECURITY AND SOCIAL DEVELOPMENT

Recent years have seen substantial changes in the approach to, and objectives of, economic development and growth. National authorities have come to recognise that development is a process which involves the continuous interaction of social and economic factors. The International Development Strategy of the 1970s[2] emphasised this as follows:

The ultimate objective of development must be to bring about sustained improvement in the well-being of the individual and bestow benefits on all . . . to bring about a more equitable distribution of income and wealth for promoting both social justice and efficiency of production, to raise substantially the level of employment, to achieve a greater degree of income security, to expand and improve facilities for education, health, nutrition, housing and social welfare, and to safeguard the environment.

In 1976 the Director-General of the ILO declared in *Employment, growth and basic needs: A one-world problem*[3] that "employment issues are intimately connected to the wider issues of poverty and inequality . . . and development planning should include, as an explicit goal, the satisfaction of an absolute level of basic needs". The keynote of the "basic needs" strategy is that satisfaction of the needs of the poor must become the core of development policies.

This evolution in thinking about the means and ends of development brings us to the crucial question: what role does social security play in social development?

Early social security schemes were designed to give working men and women better protection than lay in the Poor Law and to maintain them above the poverty line. This thread of principle, reinforced by others, has run through the development and diversification of social security programmes ever since. The result has been that many people have been able to satisfy basic needs in circumstances in which they might not otherwise have done so. Social security has not provided the whole answer to the problem of poverty, even in developed countries, but it has greatly helped.

In developing countries people enjoy less protection from social security programmes since, because a smaller proportion of the population is in the formal wage-paid sector, the programmes generate less benefit potential. In most developing countries there is a steady migration from rural areas to towns, with the consequent problems of urban unemployment and overcrowding — problems which are outside the scope of regular social security programmes, as are the problems of rural areas themselves which have been discussed in Chapter 2. Nevertheless there is an opportunity for the national authorities to use the resources of the social security administration in aid of a wider plan for medical care, maternity and public health services: an opportunity which, when it is taken, has an impact on social development and on the quality of life in rural areas.

SOCIAL SECURITY AND INCOME REDISTRIBUTION

It almost goes without saying that if the broad social effect of a social security programme is to improve the quality of life, the broad economic effect is to redistribute income. Winston Churchill characterised social insurance as "bringing the magic of averages to the rescue of the millions".

The way in which income is redistributed by social security schemes can be described under two headings, "horizontal" and "vertical".

127

Horizontal redistribution of income is implicit in every kind of social security scheme, whether it is operating on the insurance principle or on the principle of solidarity between the fit worker and the injured worker, the active employee and the retired employee, or the family with children and the person with none. On the one side are the people from whom the contributions or taxes are collected on a regular and continuing basis, and on the other are those to whom the money is transferred in the contingency which the scheme caters for.

Usually the horizontal transfer is made only within the group of people who are covered by the benefits which the scheme provides. Where, as is often the case in a developing country, that group is only a part of the population, the financial arrangement is a social insurance fund and the actual redistributive effect may be quite small in relation to the national economy. Where a social security programme has achieved a state-wide coverage for benefits, the scale of transfer of funds can be considerable, as evidenced in table 9 earlier in this chapter.

A provident fund does not redistribute income in that broad sense. Its only effect of this kind is to transfer the employer's contribution to the benefit of the employee, as though it were deferred pay.

Vertical redistribution, or the transfer of means and purchasing power from higher-income groups to persons of more modest wealth, is an objective widely pursued through various economic and social policies. Obvious ways of doing this are by direct taxation and by controls on prices, incomes and profits; indirect ways are through food subsidies and policies in relation to education, health, child welfare, municipal programmes and public housing projects. A considerable measure of vertical redistribution can be achieved in the operation of social security.

In theory, the scope for such redistribution ought to be greater in developing countries where the disparity of per capita income between rural sectors and urbanised workers in mines and factories is most marked. But these are the very places where social security in its early stages is limited to the wage-paid sector and does not yet have the possibility of using its corrective function. Hence there is a strong case, on economic grounds, for extending the coverage of social security, for using conventional systems of benefits financed through taxation or social insurance funds instead of provident funds, and for abolishing the prevalent practice of excluding the lowest-paid categories, such as casual workers and domestic servants, from coverage.

The two points in the system at which discrimination can be exercised in favour of the lower-paid or underprivileged are at the collection of contributions and in the formula by which benefit rates are determined. Most schemes divide the workers' contributions between the workers and their employers, as a matter of course, and many charge a smaller proportion to the workers on low wages or, in the case of very low-paid workers, charge the whole contribution to the employer. When some schemes collected wage-related contributions by using insurance stamps in a range of values related to the midpoint of successive wage-bands, it was common practice to impose a relatively lower percentage contribution on the lowest wage-band and a relatively higher percentage contribution on the upper wage-bands.

There are various ways in which the rate of old-age pension (and, in consequence, of other long-term benefits) may be weighted in favour of the lower-paid worker as against the contributor in the higher ranges of wages or salary. The simplest way is to prescribe a minimum and a maximum rate of pension throughout the scheme. Another way is for the award to be made up of a fixed element and a variable element so computed as to attain the desired result.

Although the main economic feature of social security programmes may be the power to redistribute income within their field, thus conforming to one of the broad objectives of social protection and social justice, such redistribution is only one of their secondary functions. Even in industrialised countries with comprehensive social security programmes, a much greater redistributive effect is achieved by direct taxation and by the management of other spending programmes. In many developing countries, policies designed to bring about more equitable distribution of income are increasingly to be found in the areas of fiscal intervention, land reform, selective subsidies and direct welfare measures to benefit the lowest-income groups.

THE EFFECT OF SOCIAL SECURITY CONTRIBUTIONS

Chapter 12 describes how the means required to run a social security scheme are found, whether from separately identifiable sources or from the general revenue. The contributory system is of such long standing that it is almost traditional and it may be asked: what are the economic effects of meeting the cost of social security in this way? Although a definitive answer is not possible, the question can be considered from various points of view.

Effect on consumption

The effects of changes in the rate of social security contributions on the household budget are probably minimal. The authorities are usually able to explain away any increase in terms of "a few cigarettes a week". The impact of the introduction of a contributory insurance scheme or provident fund with an appreciable contribution element, say 5 per cent of wages, is more marked, but is seen not so much in a drop in consumer demand as in pressure for a compensatory increase in wages or for an existing non-statutory benefit scheme to be wound up.

In any discussion of the effect of workers' contributions on consumption, it is essential to take the net effect of contributions and benefits together. The family budget which bears a relatively moderate social security charge in normal times is compensated by a substantial amount of benefit when wages fail. The demand for food and other essential goods is sustained over good times and bad, even if the demand for clothing and minor luxuries falls away. Thus, the existence of social security helped to protect the purchasing power of persons unemployed in the economic recession of the late 1970s and the 1980s.

A specific effect of workers' contributions on consumption is that there will be an increased demand for pharmaceutical products after a sickness insurance scheme is introduced.

Undoubtedly the economic position of pensioners and their influence as a group of consumers has markedly changed in the years since the Second World War. This is due to the increase not only in their numbers but in their disposable income — and pensioners as a class spend their income; they are consumers rather than savers. More old people now lead independent lives instead of being dependants in the homes of their children. A whole section of industry has grown up to cater for pensioners' holidays and other entertainment and, in any media discussion on the cost of living, families and pensioners are considered separately.

Effect on production, wages and employment

The status of the employee's social security contribution in the economic scheme of things is straightforward: it is an element of wages, it reduces take-home pay and it affects current and prospective purchasing power. The status of the so-called employer's contribution is more complex: it is part of a package of costs, profits, prices, wages, turnover and taxes. So there is a pronounced difference of views on the effect of any increase in the employer's contribution. Although an increase in the employee's contribution can be measured in terms of "a few cigarettes a week", the same increase in the employer's contribution can amount to a considerable sum, particularly in labour-intensive enterprises.

Will employers regard an increase in the employer's contribution as part of the cost of production and shift it on to their customers in the form of a higher price? Will they increase their output, reduce their unit costs and hope to hold their prices? Will they shift the increase back to their workers in the next round of wage-bargaining? Will they reflect that because the increase is tax-deductible, it isn't quite as bad as it looks? The inevitable outcome is usually some combination of all these elements, depending upon the state of the market for various products, the availability or shortage of labour, the capital cost of changing production methods, and the bargaining power of trade unions.

Where the employer's contribution is allowable as a deduction from gross income for tax purposes, a substantial part of the cost is transferred to the community and becomes a concealed state subsidy to the social insurance fund. Where an earmarked tax is levied on selected goods or services to finance a social security scheme — a practice followed in some countries — there will usually be secondary, socially desirable, reasons for such a tax. For example, a special tax on luxury goods may curb conspicuous consumption in a developing country. By contrast, such a duty levied on food articles, fuel, city transportation services or other necessities is regressive, bearing more heavily on the family budgets of poorer people.

There are different views on the effect of social security costs on production and employment. Benefits are in general spent to meet current needs and it is argued that the volume of benefits (including family benefits and pensions) sustains a heightened demand for goods and services and a higher level of employment. Not so, runs the counter-argument, which holds that the cost of providing these benefits reduces profitability and the volume of employment and encourages employers to substitute capital-intensive mechanical systems. A reasonable approach is to appreciate that social security is only a part of the total labour cost, which is itself only a part (though a large part) of the total production cost. The labour cost comprises direct wages, social charges related to employment and to safety, health and welfare provisions, and other items including social security contributions. Thus, social security contributions may not in themselves be particularly significant, even if they are fixed, inescapable and non-negotiable.

If manipulating the contribution sources of social security is unlikely to have a significant effect on production and employment, the power of pension funds is regarded as a major factor in economic affairs. In many developing countries a good part of the capital requirements of enterprises is met from savings mobilised by public authorities from a variety of sources, not least from funded social insurance schemes and provident funds.

SOCIAL SECURITY, SAVINGS AND INVESTMENT

Social security programmes accumulate financial surpluses to an extent which depends upon the kind of scheme and the method of financing applied. These surpluses can be considerable in social insurance pension schemes and are largest of all in provident funds. They also constitute an important element of internal savings. Where old-age benefit schemes have been established in developing countries, the age structure of the covered population is heavily biased towards youth. With relatively few beneficiaries for a generation or so, surpluses must therefore be large. In the case of provident funds, such surpluses are very large indeed.

Table 10.   Savings[1] from social security expressed as a percentage of national savings[2] in selected industrialised and developing countries in 1977 (in millions of national currency)

Country	Savings from social security	National savings	Savings from social security as a percentage of national savings
Africa			
Mauritius [3]	32.61	1 020.00	3.2
Morocco	249.87	6 160.00 [4]	4.1
Tunisia	56.73	255.10	22.2
Zambia	30.34	199.30	15.2
America			
Brazil	1 904.80	345 137.00	0.6
Canada	3 774.70	569.00	17.5
Costa Rica	414.90	3 308.50	12.5
Panama [3]	45.79	291.30	15.7
United States	20 929.00	91 634.00	22.8
Asia			
India [5]	9 617.60	99 620.00	9.7
Japan	4 708 900.00	37 809 000.00	12.5
Europe			
Belgium	3 507.20	353 695.00	1.0
France	6 841.70	205 968.00	3.3
Norway	2 163.90	12 555.00	17.2
United Kingdom	1 786.00	9 508.00	18.8

[1] Difference between social security receipts and expenditure in ILO: *The Cost of Social Security: Tenth International Inquiry, 1975-1977* (Geneva, 1981).   [2] United Nations: *Yearbook of National Accounts Statistics, 1978* (New York, 1979).   [3] Figures relate to 1976.   [4] Including consumption of fixed capital.   [5] Figures relate to 1975.

In the discussion in Chapter 12 on the techniques of financing pension schemes it has been explained that these surpluses, and provident fund surpluses, must be invested according to the normal criteria of safety, liquidity, yield and effective contribution to socio-economic progress. The relevant legislation usually requires that investment should be made in government securities, or at least under the direction of an investment committee on which the Ministry of Finance and the central, or development, banking institution are strongly represented.

Besides the cumulative effect of the central financial system, the routine operation of a social security scheme throws up a surplus (or deficit) at the end of each year. From international surveys the figures shown in table 10 on the financial aspects of social security in selected industrialised and developing countries can be produced.

Table 10 shows that the savings from social security schemes in relation to overall national savings are quite impressive in a number of industrialised countries and in some developing countries. For certain developing countries, although the savings ratios are not so impressive, they are by no means insignificant in absolute terms. The social security schemes of some industrialised countries do make a large contribution to national savings but it must be borne in mind that these schemes, being more comprehensive in content and coverage, play a much greater role in their national economies than do those in the developing countries.

Although the compulsory character of social security savings is not often highlighted, the national authorities in most developing countries count on funds generated by their social security schemes as an important source of savings for capital formation and investment. In periods of economic hardship and inflation, probably the only savings generated by the fixed income groups are in the form of provident fund and pension insurance contributions. During such times, people on fixed incomes might default on their life insurance premiums, but they will not easily avoid their social security obligations as their contributions are deducted at source before payment of wages. From the political angle, many national authorities find it easier and more expedient to use funds from pension schemes and provident funds than to operate through direct taxation.

The element of forced saving implicit in the financing of social security may even be regarded by the participants as a welcome imposition, provided that adequate safeguards are taken to ensure that the real worth of the participants' savings is protected against inflation and that reasonable returns are provided in the pattern of social security benefits.

In most developing countries, although the national authorities responsible for development planning regard the funds generated by social security schemes as dependable sources of capital, they might not recognise social security as a sector amenable to planning. The most common arguments are that the techniques of allocative planning applied to other social sectors like health, education and housing are irrelevant because social security has its built-in structures involving transfers rather than managed expenditure; and that the targets and achievements under social security do not lend themselves to precise quantification as compared to other social sectors.

However, in recent years, there has been a growing consensus that social security should be integrated with development planning. National planning agencies have come to believe that the resources (and potential resources) generated by social security schemes are dependable sources of capital with which public expenditure under the plans can be financed. In fact, some development economists seem to favour the introduction and development of social security long-term benefit schemes (including provident funds) as an effective means of mobilising domestic savings. Given the appropriate financial systems with contribution and benefit structures, there should be little reason to expect major fluctuations in the resources accruing from the schemes and the planners can, when applying their techniques, take into account savings from social security.

With a forced saving system ready to hand in the social security scheme, some national authorities might be tempted to overlook the importance of having reasonable returns from the investment of social security reserves. There is a good case for devising, and insisting on, public policies designed to safeguard the adequacy of returns on social security investments and to protect their nominal and real value through flexible and realistic rates of interest and monetary correction, or through indexation.

Social security institutions, especially in the developing countries, find themselves confronted with hard options as they attempt to reconcile the usually established criteria of investment with the available investment opportunities. The criteria themselves might appear mutually incompatible in some typical national situations. Steadily mounting inflation has at times made it impossible to ensure either genuine security for social security savings or satisfactory yields. Some investments that might be avoided in principle according to accepted standards (for example, investments in real estate) might prove to be the safest and the most profitable. But, in an inflationary situation characterised by speculative movements, such investments might be incompatible with rules laid down by national financial authorities.

Quite apart from that, pressure might also be experienced from both official and non-official quarters to attract the social security funds. Public policy guidelines ought not to be so rigid as to preclude investment in socially desirable projects. It ought to be possible to draw up national priorities, assigning sufficient weight to projects such as hospitals, schools and low-cost housing, so that a part of the funds can be used in a manner compatible with national policies on the equitable redistribution of income.

SOCIAL SECURITY IN TIMES OF ECONOMIC PRESSURE

In normal times of steady growth, unhindered by abrupt fluctuations in national economic variables, social security systems are well able to meet their obligations to their clients and to maintain the general credibility of their financial systems. When designing the financial systems, and especially the contribution and benefit structure, the planners take into account predictable changes in the demographic and economic conditions and build in safety devices to contain these changes, within a reasonable margin of error. However, during periods of severe economic crisis marked by persistently high levels of inflation, continuing recession and widespread unemployment, the financial mechanisms are subjected to such severe strain as to impair their capacity to meet their obligations.

If wages rise with inflationary pressure, and if contribution rates are related to the level of wages, a rise in the yield from contributions would be expected. In practice, however, the rise will not be realised in full because of the reduction in the numbers of persons in employment. Any specific increase in the rate of contribution has to be nicely judged, since it is effectively a cut in wages at a sensitive time.

Financing social security programmes out of general revenue is, as has been shown throughout this book, standard practice in many countries. Social security schemes with a restricted coverage are normally expected to be self-supporting, but frequently they enjoy an element of subsidy from the general revenue. The closer contributory schemes approach universal coverage, the nearer the contributions approximate to a general tax. The question of allocating further funds to the social security programme in an emergency thus becomes one not of technical propriety but of policy and of priorities at a time when taxable capacity is straitened and when there are many competing demands on it. The question can only be resolved with reference to the particular arguments advanced by the parties concerned at the time.

Another area in which broad economic considerations can confront administrators with difficult policy decisions is that of demographic change. According to one shock estimate, the ratio of social security contributors to beneficiaries in the United States fell from 16.5:1 to 3.2:1 between 1950 and 1981. The estimate envisages that two contributors will be carrying each beneficiary in the year 2030. If this were to be so, social security would have become a major element indeed in the national economy.

It may be, as some have claimed, that the successful results which social security has achieved and is consistently delivering as an economic weapon in the contingencies which it has so far confronted, have encouraged an exaggerated view of its ultimate possibilities. However, the basic principles and structures of social security have emerged with enhanced strength and authority from economic crises in the past and may profit equally from the problems of the 1980s. Problems in social security financing in the developed world could have a dampening effect on the enthusiasm of the developing countries that have the capacity and political will to introduce economically feasible programmes. Instead of falling into a mood of undue caution and timidity, the developing countries should be able to profit from the experiences of the industrialised countries by systematically planning and implementing programmes which match their prevailing and emerging economic conditions and by ensuring that the real objectives and purposes of social security are met.

Notes

[1] ILO: *Project findings and recommendations: Employment injury benefits and feasibility of providing age benefits*, Report by J. Grieve (Geneva, doc. ETH/70/005), Appendix A, paragraph 4.

[2] Resolution No. 2626(XXV), 24 October 1970, in United Nations: *Resolutions adopted by the General Assembly during its twenty-fifth session, 15 September-17 December 1970*, Official Records, Supplement No. 28 (A/8028)

[3] ILO: *Employment, growth and basic needs: A one-world problem*, Report of the Director-General of the International Labour Office to the Tripartite World Conference on Employment, Income Distribution and Social Progress and the International Division of Labour (Geneva, 1976).

ADMINISTRATION OF SOCIAL SECURITY 14

ADMINISTRATIVE STRUCTURES

There is no standard pattern or recommended model for the administration of social security. Indeed, it would be surprising if there were since, as has been shown, most of the structures at present in use grew up with a minimum of positive planning for a combination of reasons — historical, political and social. The earliest employment injury schemes were administered by employers, commercial insurance companies and the courts of law, and this pattern continues successfully in many places even today. Other early structures took the Bismarckian pattern, where the social insurance legislation provided for sickness and pensions institutes to be managed by representatives of the contributors themselves, a principle which was written into the Sickness Insurance (Industry) Convention, 1927 (No. 24), and the Sickness Insurance (Agriculture) Convention, 1927 (No. 25), which concerned workers in industry and commerce, domestic servants and agricultural workers. Examples of this localised structure are still to be found in many countries.

There are countries, too, where the gradual achievement of near-universal coverage of the population has been accompanied by the gradual creation of a comprehensive single institution to manage the social security programme. There are yet other countries which, profiting by example, have established their social security programmes under a single national management from the outset.

In this chapter the characteristic features of the kind of administrative structure which controls and directs a developed social security structure at the top level are discussed. How social security activity is made effective locally, at the point of delivery of the service, is indicated, together with the importance of co-ordination and communication throughout all operations. First of all, however, consideration is given to a feature of social security administration which has conditioned its shape in many countries — the collection and recording of contributions.

COLLECTION AND RECORDING OF CONTRIBUTIONS

All social insurance and provident fund schemes must identify their contributors and make sure that the contributions are properly brought to account in the central records of the institution. These consist not only of individual records of contributions paid (numbers of contributions, or length of contribution periods in the case of an insurance scheme; and cash amounts in a provident fund) but also of alphabetical indexes to assist identification, prevent duplication of accounts and, as a by-product, provide statistical data of the covered population.

Such records are an essential feature of provident funds, and of insurance schemes which provide long-term benefits after qualifying periods which extend over many years; and they must be centralised because contributors may move from employer to employer, and between different parts of the country, during their working lives. It is not usually necessary to refer to the central records when certifying a claim for short-term benefit; it will suffice to inquire of the employer about recent wages or contributions; but in some systems the rate of benefit depends on a 12-month record during the previous two years or so. In provident funds every contribution must be exactly recorded in order for it to be repaid in due course, with interest.

Initially the institution can identify potential contributors from taxation and licensing records, local trades directories, labour department files, and so on. Employees are registered through employers. Normally the identification data will be the name, date and place of birth, signature or fingerprint or photograph. With the increasing use of electronic equipment, codified identity numbers have become almost universal. Furthermore, a personal number that embodies some statistical information can be useful in various contexts.

Almost always the employees' contributions are deducted from wages and are paid over, with the employer's contributions, to the institution. Most schemes also collect from self-employed persons as individuals on a voluntary or a compulsory basis. The method of payment and collection has to be flexible to suit the circumstances. Earlier schemes made much use of the stamped card method, but this has been largely superseded by variations of the pay-roll method.

1. In the stamped card method, the employer holds a card for each employee. A special stamp representing the employer's and the employee's contribution — the latter having been deducted from wages — is regularly affixed to it. Stamps are bought from the social security institution or through the post office. Cards are current for a year. At the end of the year, having been exchanged for fresh cards, they are used as posting documents to bring the central records of the contributors up to date. The method was originally devised when flat-rate contributions gave title to flat-rate benefits and it is not easily

adaptable to the collection of wage-related contributions from monthly pay-rolls. Its merit is simplicity and some schemes use it for individual and isolated contributors, such as self-employed persons or domestic servants.

2.   Basically, under the pay-roll method, the employers remit the contributions direct to the institution at regular intervals. Usually remittances are not sent in less frequently than once a month, though the nominal roll giving details of the individual workers and the amounts due might be rendered quarterly. These personal details are then transferred to the individual central records either manually or by electronic input, as the case may require.

The social security planners have to examine a number of factors before constructing their procedure for collection. One such factor is how information on the qualifying conditions for benefit should be dealt with. Depending on the formula written into the law, it may be easier to rely upon information which is regularly fed into central records — or it may be more convenient to intercept some of this information at the local office. Certain procedures may be most economical where the government itself is the largest employer; others may be demanded to suit large private employers with their own mechanised pay-roll systems; yet others may be appropriate where employment is widely spread in smaller pockets. Whatever procedure is adopted for collecting and recording personal details of employers and covered persons, the confidentiality of these records must be safeguarded. The principal legislation usually includes a section imposing on all officials and staff a duty of secrecy in the handling of personal information, not only in this area of administration but also in the course of benefit claims work, with severe penalties for breach of this duty.

In the final analysis, the choice of a collection system is a matter of balancing the respective interests of employers and of the administration. If there is an agreed preference, the choice will be simple. If not, every effort has to be made to meet the wishes of the employers, since the imposition of a system which is disliked can only antagonise them and prejudice the operation of the social security programme.

ADMINISTERING SOCIAL SECURITY – THE VIEW FROM THE TOP

Policy formation

The existence of schemes providing protection against all, or a wide range of, contingencies necessitates close co-ordination between the branches covered and also with schemes which may be administered outside the social security sphere — for example, medical care services provided by central or local government agencies, or unemployment benefit arrangements allied to the placement services of government labour offices. Where nominally autonomous bodies administer each branch or type of contingency, the need for co-ordination is obvious — and it is all the more pressing if a number of separate administrations handle one subject such as sickness benefit. In any case the scale, or potential scale, of social security nowadays means that it must come under the policy supervision of a central government department. In most countries this is the ministry dealing with labour affairs (usually now designated "Ministry of Labour and Welfare", or "Ministry of Labour and Social Affairs", and so on). In some countries social security is included in the health portfolio. Only occasionally does one find a separate ministry of social security, but the subject may be entrusted to the finance ministry or to the ministry of the interior. In the pattern of government elsewhere there may be a "Social Security Commission".

Almost universally the central direction of social security policy — the nature of the benefits, the content of the legislation, the allocation of funds within national economic planning and other fundamental aspects of the social security programme — is now a concern of the government at ministerial level. The departmental designation may reflect the thrust or bias of a particular programme, such as its interest in co-ordinating cash benefits with treatment benefits or its integration of social insurance benefits with social assistance and welfare. Of course, whether the policy direction is located in one ministry or remains divided amongst several, any major development or change will involve wider discussion with departments of finance and legal affairs and even (as will be seen in Chapter 15) external affairs.

Top direction

The central department which is responsible for social security policy may also be responsible for implementing and administering the policy all the way down the line; the whole operation is then managed within the public service. Alternatively, the central department may retain operational responsibility for part of the programme, such as the long-term pensions branch, but may delegate other parts, such as sickness benefits, to long-standing local agencies in order for them to look after their own circle of members under the law.

In other countries, and this is on the whole a more usual arrangement, the legislation creates a parastatal body (with some such title as "Social Security Institute", "National Insurance Board", "National Social Security Fund", or similar) with legal responsibility to implement the terms of the law, thus relieving the minister, who retains portfolio responsibility, of the burden of day-to-day administration. The degree of independent action open to such a body varies: some may have the power to engage their own staff and build their own premises, others may rely on secondment from the public service and on renting accommodation from the government; some may have a free hand to invest funds, others may be subject to direction by the finance ministry. A statutory board is almost always found at the head of a contributory social insurance scheme or a provident fund. The accumulated moneys are vested in the board which acts in effect as trustee for the contributors, publishing annual reports and accounts. A board which is itself responsible for investing funds is likely to have an investment committee, formed from members experienced in this area of financial management, both workers' and employers' representatives, and experts from, for example, the finance ministry, development bank or investment consultants.

Because social insurance and provident funds work to closely defined legal rules, there is not much scope for a board to intervene in technical matters. But with social assistance, where officials have more discretion in determining the needs and resources of claimants, the board will have to give directions on policy aspects of the day-to-day administration. In either case, however, the board will have an influential voice with its parent ministry in the development of major policy matters.

Where administration is delegated to an autonomous body, it is not unusual to find a two-stage arrangement. A deliberative assembly meets at intervals — certainly once a year — to deal with the budget and to consider broader policy matters; a smaller executive committee meets more regularly and maintains contact with the permanent head of the board's staff.

Much of this, naturally, is reflected in the Social Security (Minimum Standards) Convention, 1952 (No. 102), which lays down that the member government shall accept general responsibility for the proper administration of the institutions and services concerned with social security. The Convention also requires that where the administration is delegated away from government level, the representatives of the protected persons should participate in the management or be associated with it in a representative capacity. A typical statutory board would more than fulfil this requirement, comprising both employed persons and employers, with the addition of several officials from the major government departments concerned. The worker and employer members of the board are usually elected or nominated by the trade unions and employers' organisations, respectively, or appointed by the minister after consultation with these bodies. Often the director or permanent head of the organisation supervised by the board has a seat on the board itself.

In the situation where the administration is not delegated but remains in a separate division of the responsible government department, representatives of the covered persons and of employers may be appointed to an advisory committee, not unlike the statutory board but with the simpler function of giving advice to the minister. Such a committee would advise on matters of policy or administration which the minister might refer to it or which its members might raise on their own initiative. Another way of associating the protected persons with the administration of social security is for the responsibility to be devolved in some degree from the public authorities to the trade unions.

Headquarters organisation

The shape of the organisation which serves the board, the investment committee and the director (where this is the structure of the top direction) will be dictated by the size of the covered population, the extent to which it is concentrated in a reasonably manageable area or dispersed over a larger territory and the variety and nature of the benefits to be administered. The functions to be carried out would, in a headquarters office of any size, require the director to be supported by several senior staff, notably:

(a) a finance officer, responsible for such matters as budget, accounts and internal audit;

(b) (in a social insurance, or provident fund, scheme) a contributions officer, responsible for all the procedures related to the registration of employers, employees and other contributors, for the collection of their contributions and for the maintenance of the central contribution records; and

(c) a benefits officer, similarly responsible for all benefit procedures and for appeals arrangements.

The maintenance of a central record of long-term pensioners, and the regular repetitive work of keeping their pensions in payment, lends itself to mechanical processes and is often handled by a central office. All of these functions add up to an appreciable administrative task, which increases to the formidable as schemes widen in scope and become more complicated. Apart from the technical tasks so far defined, there is the whole internal "housekeeping" job to be done: in determining the number of staff required and organising their deployment and training; the provision of working premises, furniture, stationery and equipment; the custody and control of moneys received; and the maintenance of a public relations service which will keep all interested parties informed of the progress and development of the scheme.

Some further technical matters are worth mentioning as important features of the headquarters service. One of these is statistics. The regular day-by-day or week-by-week compilation of statistics of work-flow, of contributors registered, of benefit claims received and processed and of long-term benefits in payment is not only an aid to current management but an essential source of information for the regular actuarial reviews of the health of any social insurance fund. The importance of statistics in the management of social security, both nationally and internationally, has been emphasised by the ILO in the detailed guidance given in the publication entitled *Scheme of statistical tables for the practical application of a minimum programme of social security statistics.*[1]

In a large-scale organisation, and wherever it is charged with providing medical care benefits, the headquarters would need the assistance of a medical officer to advise the staff on medical matters and to organise the medical examination of claimants for invalidity benefit and employment injury disablement benefits; and also a legal officer to handle questions of the interpretation of the law, prosecutions for non-compliance and fraud, and the organisation and procedure of appeal bodies. In a smaller organisation most of the functions of the headquarters would be combined, and in the specialist areas — medical and legal — the director would look to the appropriate government departments for assistance.

Finally, where the top direction remains within a division of a government department, the same technical functions must be carried out in relation to contributions and benefits, but other matters, notably personnel, premises and aspects of finance, will pass largely out of the control of the divisional head who will rely on other common services within the government apparatus, such as audit, staff training, public relations, printing and stationery and transport. At any level, social security operations call for specialised training, and the divisional head must be aware of the interlocking dangers of losing trained and experienced staff too easily on transfer within the government service, or of blocking the career prospects of useful officers for whom there is a restricted chance of advancement in the relatively small social security division.

ADMINISTERING SOCIAL SECURITY AT THE LOCAL LEVEL

The local office

The main task of any social security organisation is to pay benefits correctly, promptly and humanely, in accordance with the law. Everything else which it does, though very necessary, is subordinate and complementary to that. Because social security benefits are, by a well-understood intention, paid to replace lost or interrupted wages, the arrangements for payment should conform to local practice — weekly where the personal and family budgets are organised round weekly wages; perhaps less frequently where wages are customarily paid at longer intervals.

Whatever is done at the central headquarters, the effective impact of social security as a personal service has to be in the covered person's own neighbourhood, at the social security local office. Naturally, the central office is likely to have a "local office" attached to it, but the functions have to be distinguished. In a small compact island State, this may be the only local office but in any other situation there will be more — often many more — local offices so that social security facilities can be brought within reasonable reach of as much of the covered population as is practicable. The offices will be widely dispersed and can vary considerably in size. The official in charge of a medium-sized local office could have a fully articulated organisation with its own finance section; a contributions section to handle local registrations and the routine collection of contributions (and all the inquiries and problems which arise in that connection); specialist benefit sections to deal with employment injuries and long-term benefits; a rather larger section for sickness and maternity benefits and funeral grants; and the customary services for use by all sections.

The local office reproduces on its own scale the content of the central office — with two important additions. Firstly, there will be a public office and private interview facilities where members of the public can attend to register, obtain information and advice, be helped in making claims for any benefit and produce documentary evidence for inspection. Secondly, the local office will be fully equipped for the payment of cash benefits.

Cash benefits are paid in a variety of ways. They can be paid directly to the beneficiary at the public office, (and this is particularly the case with unemployment benefit, about which more is said below). Sometimes payments of sickness or other benefits may be made to an authorised representative of the beneficiary who is unable to attend at the office in person, but generally such payment is made either by mail or during a home visit by an official from the local office. Employers are sometimes required to pay benefit to any employee who is off work (perhaps along with a proportion of wages); they are then reimbursed by the local office, or the amount is credited against their liability for insurance contributions. This system of payment by the employer was once typical of family allowances but the alternative, of paying allowances directly to the mother by periodical postal order or similar instrument, is preferred by many schemes.

The continued, renewable, periodical payment of long-term benefits lends itself, as was noted above, to payment from a central office. The local office has an important role in making immediate payments of injury benefit until a disabled worker's entitlement to a disablement pension can be assessed; and in making immediate payments to a widow while her pension title is being investigated. In some developing countries where local banking or post office facilities are lacking, pensions are paid in cash by the local office from a prepared pay-list or schedule supplied monthly from the central office.

There should be a limit to the size of community for which normal local office services can be organised. For smaller communities much ingenuity must be exercised in maintaining the essential contact with covered persons, claimants and beneficiaries. Part-time offices may be manned by members of a small travelling team, or a visiting official on a day or two each week, who take claims back to the nearest town for processing; or agency arrangements may be set up with other district or local government offices. Outlying areas may be served by mobile offices. In the extreme case of a scattered island State there may be no alternative but to concentrate most of the functions of the local office upon one or two officials, who must demonstrate considerable virtuosity, and to give them as much regular support as possible.

Medical benefits

How far the social security local office becomes involved in the provision of medical care benefits depends, in part, on whether the medical side is organised on the "direct" or "indirect" system, as described in Chapter 4. The social security office may have to receive and check accounts for medical services, prescriptions and hospital care; or claims for reimbursement where covered persons have already met the full costs. In a different structure of services, a dispensary or clinic may be associated with the local office, even sharing premises and coming under common management. The situation is different again in a country which provides a public health service, organised independently of the social security programme; but, depending upon the arrangements for charges, the local office may have to ensure that immediate free medical and surgical treatment is available for victims of industrial accidents.

Compliance

Achieving and maintaining satisfactory standards of compliance with the law on contributions poses serious problems for social insurance institutions. The old-established schemes in industrial countries are not immune and follow a settled policy of prosecuting offending employers in order to promote a better general standard. Wherever social insurance schemes or provident funds are operating in developing countries, the same problems exist. The spearhead of the attack on the problem is found in the local office. The governing legislation in a contributory scheme invariably authorises the appointment of inspectors with legal power to enter any place of employment. Their main function is to make sure that all those who come within the scope of the law are duly registered and that the contribution rules are fully complied with. The inspector can require production of wages books and of all associated documents, such as stamped contribution cards and copies of periodical contribution schedules, and can interview any person about what is covered by these records.

In addition to these routine inspections, the inspector will carry a varied volume of case work which has arisen in the local area. The inspector's duty is to sort out the problems through discussion with employers. It is a measure of the success of the inspector's efforts that this case-load should contain as few instances as possible of employers in such serious default that legal proceedings against them are being prepared.

Unemployment benefit

Unemployment benefit could be paid at the social security local office. However, as claimants invariably have to attend the employment exchange or placement office of the labour department in order to prove their eligibility for the benefit, it is that office which takes over the payment of benefit under the social security programme. A close liaison is naturally maintained between these two local offices because questions of fitness, unfitness and incapacity for work, and questions on the borderline of age, invalidity and retirement, may have to be resolved in respect of the same claimant.

CO-ORDINATION AND COMMUNICATION WITHIN A UNIFIED ADMINISTRATION

Where the several branches of a social security programme (or most of them) are entrusted to a single institution, the size and shape of the central office may vary, and the number of local offices may vary, but both ends of the structure must be there and, if the institution is to serve the covered population effectively, there must be smooth and regular communication in many different ways from the centre to the public reception office and, indeed, beyond that. Every medium of communication is called upon at some point. For example, the printed word in leaflets, stock forms and staff instructions; the spoken word in interviews and conferences; radio, television, press advertising, posters, cinema slides, to reach persons who do not call at local offices; and telephone, teleprinter and electronic data transmission for internal liaison.

Up to a point, the better the available communications media, the greater the case for keeping the administration centralised. In this way, a mass of routine operations can be performed in bulk, with advantages of economy due to size, and the operations can be performed by mechanised or electronic means when appropriate. Beyond a certain point, however, the sheer scale of communication facilities may dictate the creation of an intermediate level of administration, with district or regional offices handling some functions delegated from the centre, together with some benefit functions, such as medical examinations, or appeals, on behalf of a group of local offices.

Staff aspects

As soon as an organisation has two or more local offices each devoted to the same function, steps must be taken to ensure that they carry out that function in the same way. There are two reasons for this: firstly, to simplify the handling of business when case papers (or, for that matter, officials) are transferred between offices; and secondly so that the public will have a uniform standard of service in different local areas. There are also two principal ways of achieving this result: one is by the use of formalised, internal written instructions and procedure sheets; and the other is by regular and systematic staff training. Systems which are based on the precise rules of social insurance or provident fund methods are reasonably easy to standardise in the former way, while in the more discretionary atmosphere of social assistance administration the inculcation of principles through carefully prepared staff training is of greater importance.

Management aspects

A widely dispersed organisation needs a system of internal written instructions; it also needs line managers who are familiar with the overall doctrine and patterns of management. The rendering of regular state-of-business reports to the central office is an obvious and necessary routine link. More important to the general health and efficiency of the organisation is the nurturing of personal contact between the director and senior staff at headquarters with the corresponding people at the local offices. Without this, the outstations can feel very isolated. Within sensible limits of cost-effectiveness, controlling staff have to reserve part of their time to visit the other offices; and periodical conferences of local office managers, at which the broader aspects, aims and achievements of the organisation can be discussed, are a feature of successful social security programmes.

Contributions aspects

In contributory systems, probably the most sensitive area in which smooth co-ordination has to be achieved is between employers and the local office, and between the local office and the central records. The use of preprinted schedules, on which the employer simply has to add or delete names of employees and to insert the amounts of contributions, is one way of easing communications; and it is vital that there is the least delay, consistent with accuracy, in updating the individual records of each covered person, whether from quarterly schedules or annual stamp cards. (The record may not be wanted for 40 years, but errors and inconsistencies must be identified and dealt with promptly in the meantime.) With a stamp card system, the annual bulk exchange of cards and their processing, all the way from employers' premises, through local offices, to the central record office and archives, should be organised with almost military precision. Much ingenuity has been put into devising computer processes in this area, even to the extent of receiving employers' contribution returns as an output from their wages computers, in a form that may be fed directly into the computerised social security records. Other systems seek to simplify the employer's task by collecting the social security contribution with pay-as-you-earn income tax in a combined operation.

Benefit aspects

In a well-conceived and well-designed social security organisation, the teamwork of the whole system is focused ultimately upon the benefits staff in the local office. Ideally, any legislation will be so drafted that the qualifying conditions can be verified and satisfied without time-wasting correspondence. In order to achieve this, the executive staff and the policy and legal experts must be brought into the planning process at an early stage. Internal procedures should require the minimum reference (if any) from the local office to central records before a claim is certified and means should be devised to make the reference procedure as rapid as possible. For this, some offices enjoy the ultimate refinement of immediate access through electronic visual display units. Finance procedures should be so designed that the local office always has ready means of cash payment to hand for its regular claims load and for emergencies. The in-office training programme should be so applied that, given an emergency such as an epidemic, almost any other activity of the local office can be suspended while available staff concentrate on benefits work and on the service to the public to which the whole organisation is dedicated.

ASSISTANCE SCHEMES, PUBLIC
SERVICE OR UNIVERSAL SCHEMES

Assistance schemes and public service or universal schemes of benefit are not concerned with employers, as such, nor do they involve the collection of contributions. The cost of the benefits is borne by the State or, in some cases, by local authorities and the finance comes from national or local taxation. It will be seen, therefore, that the internal arrangements of the social security organisation can be much more simple than those for social insurance or provident fund schemes.

The absolute right to benefit may be reserved to nationals born within the country concerned. Others, non-nationals and nationals born abroad, may be subject to a residence condition. To be awarded benefit under a social assistance scheme, or anything more than the standard basic pension under a public service or universal scheme, the claimants have to satisfy the authorities that their means are below the level set by the legislation. In these circumstances, as has been noted earlier, the investigating and awarding officials have an extra measure of discretion and this must qualify the nature and content of their training, supervision and methods of working.

APPEALS; AUTOMATION

This chapter would not be complete without a fuller mention of two subjects to which passing reference has been made.

Convention No. 102 stipulates that every claimant shall have a right of appeal in case of refusal of benefit or complaint as to its quality or quantity. The Convention does not specify any particular avenue of appeal: some countries use their ordinary courts; others constitute social security benefit tribunals or use existing arrangements under their labour legislation. Where tribunals are used, these often consist of a legal chairman and two members drawn from lists nominated by workers' and employers' organisations respectively. The Convention makes two reservations: in a country where medical care services are administered by a government department, complaints about medical care benefit may be reserved for investigation by the appropriate authority; and in any case where social security benefit is initially awarded by a tribunal on which covered persons are represented, there need be no further right of appeal. The later Invalidity, Old-Age and Survivors' Benefits Convention, 1967 (No. 128), adds that claimants shall have the right to be represented or assisted by a qualified person of their own choice or, for example, by a delegate from their trade union — a right which is usually accorded whatever benefit is concerned.

The electronic computer provides a means of collecting a mass of routine information, processing it and storing it economically. More and more social security institutions are turning to this as a most useful tool and it is no longer true that small schemes cannot benefit from an installation, since models which suit all types and degrees of application are available. The usefulness of a computer is not confined to its record-keeping and storage facilities; it is versatile enough to be able to adapt to virtually any technical and managerial aspect of social security, computing accurately and speedily, and providing information to assist in planning, research, statistics, finance, unit costs of administration, paying benefits and reconciling payments.

The purchase or hire of a computer will not, of course, automatically overcome problems which stem from poor basic organisation or inefficiency of administration. Only after a sound manual system of operation has been devised and is running efficiently is it the right time to consider transferring it to a computer. Indeed, so much time must be devoted to the planning, designing, ordering and installing of a computer system that efficient manual systems are essential to keep the social security system going in the meantime.

Developing countries face other difficulties when they contemplate the advantages of automation. Higher policy considerations may rule that labour-intensive methods should be used instead of machine processes, wherever possible. The use of scarce foreign currency may have to be authorised for buying or renting machines and for the hire of foreign technicians. Special problems surround the training of local staff in programming and operating the machines and the retention of staff in the organisation once they are trained. Some of these difficulties may be obviated if "time-sharing" on an existing government installation is adopted, but still much background study and careful groundwork is essential before the visible security of manual records is abandoned for the expected efficiency of the computer. Where time-sharing is resorted to, care must be taken to protect the secrecy of the personal details stored in the computer against unauthorised access by persons not subject to the statutory sanctions mentioned earlier in this chapter.

Note

[1] Extracted from *International Review on Actuarial and Statistical Problems of Social Security* (Geneva, ISSA), No. 8, 1962, and published in Rome by Tipografia del Senato del Dott. G. Bardi (1964).

SPECIAL ARRANGEMENTS FOR MIGRANT WORKERS 15

ACROSS THE FRONTIERS

Quite early in the development of social security those countries with a maritime sector found it necessary and natural to look outward, extending their coverage beyond their own borders by including the masters and crew members of merchant ships. A country would take responsibility for ships that were registered there, or whose owner or manager had a place of business there; would generally register its own nationals or residents; and would make special arrangements to collect contributions and to pay benefit where, for example, a seaman was hospitalised in a foreign country. Such workers were not migrants, however, and indeed the special arrangements invariably excluded from cover any non-nationals who were not resident in the country.

It was a small step beyond that when social security schemes arranged to retain within their coverage persons who went abroad to continue their employment in another country — such as commercial travellers, or construction workers sent out on a foreign contract. Their compulsory cover was usually continued for a limited period, say 12 months, to bridge the gap which might otherwise open up in their social security record.

In general, however, once people moved to another country, whether or not they took up employment, then, in the absence of any international agreement, they lost the social security cover which they had enjoyed (though if they had been covered under a social insurance scheme they might be allowed to continue payment voluntarily for pension). Of course they would come within the cover of any social security programme in the new country; but they might find themselves up against restrictive rules on nationality and residence; they would have to serve new qualifying periods of employment or contribution before coming into benefit; they might lose any entitlement at all to benefit for dependants who had not accompanied them; and some of those same disadvantages might await them if they later returned to the country which they had left. Such difficulties clearly demanded, from the standpoints both of justice and of social protection, the creation of appropriate international measures to safeguard the social security of migrant workers.

First of all reciprocal agreements were made by a pair of neighbouring countries or by countries with similar social security arrangements and movement of an appreciable number of people between them. From the beginning of the century such bilateral agreements multiplied − first in regard to workmen's compensation and pensions and then in the larger field of social security generally − until by the late 1950s Europe was covered by a network of agreements and others reached out, literally, around the world. The ILO naturally welcomed and encouraged the development. Its original Constitution committed the Organisation to the principle that rules laid down in any country should guarantee fair economic treatment to all workers legally resident in that country; the Preamble, as amended in 1946, recognises that it is urgent to improve working conditions in general and especially those affecting the interests of foreign workers.

The steady growth of national social security legislation since the Second World War, the increasing numbers of workers who are moving, not only seasonally, from country to country, and the way in which international organisation is developing at every level has led to more attention being paid to the protection of migrants. Wherever a number of countries are co-ordinating social, commercial and employment policies, bilateral agreements on social security are being replaced by multilateral agreements linking the several legislations concerned and incidentally encouraging the wider adoption of improvements initiated in any one country. The following brief summary of this development is devoted first to the common principles on which all of the instruments are based and then to Conventions of the ILO and other multilateral Conventions in the social security field.

BASIC PRINCIPLES OF SOCIAL SECURITY FOR MIGRANT WORKERS

The terms of social security agreements which are designed to reconcile the content of two or more sets of national legislation are bound to vary widely, but one can in general recognise five basic principles at work:

1. *Equality of treatment.* The immigrant worker should have, as far as possible, the same rights and obligations as a regular resident of the same age, sex, civil status and relevant social security qualification.

2. *Determination of applicable legislation.* There should be no room for doubt as to which specific law governs the social security protection of the migrant worker.

3. *Maintenance of acquired rights.* Any right to benefit, or paid-up

prospective right, should be guaranteed to the migrant in either territory, even if it has been acquired in the other.

4. *Maintenance of rights in course of acquisition.* Where a right to benefit is conditional upon the completion of a qualifying period, account should be taken of periods served by the migrant worker in each country.

5. *Payment of benefits abroad.* There should be no restriction on the payment, in any of the countries concerned, of benefits for which the migrant has qualified in any of the others or, for example, on the payment of family benefits in one country while the migrant is working in another.

The agreement is first spelled out in as much detail as is considered necessary by the parties to it — countries must, of course, take the content of their national legislation into account. It is then up to each country to put the agreement into force, making such modifications in the terms of its own law as are essential for that purpose and for the recognition of the legitimate interests of the migrant workers and of any peculiarities in their conditions of work, their personal situation and their family circumstances. The interests of the migrants are in general equated with the advantages enjoyed by the nationals with whom they are working. The procedures used in securing for the migrant worker benefits which might not otherwise have been payable will naturally prevent any duplication of payment which might have resulted if the laws concerned had been applied independently. In this sense, social security agreements observe a rule of equality. The demonstration of fairness and impartiality within a common level of social security protection, applicable to all workers irrespective of origin or nationality, can only be favourable to the persons concerned in the long run.

While not disturbing the essential content of particular national laws, the principal objective of the agreement is co-ordination: the elimination of any obstacle in the way of the application of these laws on the one hand and, on the other, such modification of their effects as to guarantee to migrant workers complete and continuous protection on the basis of effective equality. Co-ordination of laws is to be distinguished from harmonisation, which would imply the wholesale amendment of the national laws so as to impose a common pattern. There is no doubt, however, that co-ordination eventually has some indirect effects on the contents of laws. It sets in motion co-operation between national authorities and this leads in turn to a better understanding of common problems of social security protection.

Equality of treatment

The first principle to which social security agreements give effect is equality of treatment. The starting-point in the preparation of any reciprocal agreement must be that migrant workers should have the same rights and obligations under the law and should receive benefits on the same terms as national workers in the country of immigration.

The importance of this principle has increased considerably with the development of social security systems. In the original concept of social insurance, which still bore the mark of private insurance techniques, there was little or no discrimination on grounds of nationality because the employee's right to benefit flowed directly from payment of a contribution. Such discrimination has become more frequent in social security schemes where the relationship between contributions and the right to benefit has been weakened. This is due most notably to the advent of national systems which are financed not so much from individual contributions as from general tax revenues. Accordingly, citizenship or nationality and residence conditions have appeared, governing both the obligation to be insured and access to benefit.

This unfavourable development, occurring at the same time as the progressive improvement in the protection given by most national systems and the remarkable increase in migration of workers after the Second World War, led to a restatement, in the Equality of Treatment (Social Security) Convention, 1962 (No. 118), of the principle which had been one of the main purposes and merits of earlier agreements. The principle is so important that it has been applied generally to all foreigners, refugees and stateless persons.

Determination of the applicable legislation

The second principle seeks to guarantee that in all cases migrant workers will be protected under a specific predetermined law. For this purpose the social security agreements either identify the relevant laws or contain provisions for deciding which specific legislation must be applied to migrant workers in any given situation. This is true in the ordinary case of employment within the jurisdiction of a single country and also in the special cases of particular categories of workers, such as those detached for service abroad, workers who travel and carry out their work in two or more countries and seafarers. In the absence of clear and precise international rules, there could be a situation which required the simultaneous application of two or more conflicting laws, or which appeared to fall outside any relevant legislation.

Some kind of international regulation is necessary in the interests of migrant workers, therefore, to ensure that there is complete protection, immediately available, wherever the worker may be found for the time being. Except in regard to voluntary insurance to enable people to maintain their qualification for old-age benefit, it is not usual to permit the partial application of different branches of the relevant national laws, at least not in the agreements concluded between countries with highly developed systems of social security. Such a separation by branches would be contrary to the unified character of some of those systems and would be likely to cause greater administrative complications than any advantages arising from it would warrant.

For employed persons, the test most often used to determine which national law should apply is the place where the work is done, regardless of what country the worker resides in or where the undertaking which employs the worker has its headquarters. According to this rule, migrant workers are covered by the social security law of the country to which they go to carry out their regular or seasonal work, even though they may continue to reside in their country of origin.

The law applicable to self-employed persons may be determined either in the same way — with regard to the place where they follow their occupation — or with regard to their place of residence.

Special rules may have to be laid down for particular categories of migrant workers to whom the general rules cannot reasonably be applied. Such rules vary according to the country in question and according to the nature and working conditions of the category concerned. Commercial travellers and construction workers sent out on a foreign contract have already been mentioned; international transport workers are another example of those whose employment may take them to several countries in succession. The general rule which establishes which country's legislation is to apply could be either the location of the headquarters of the undertaking which employs the workers or the residence of the persons concerned. In the case of seamen, however, it may be a question of the flag or registration of their ship.

A review of existing social security agreements reveals that the methods of determining the legislation applicable in any given case are diverse and complex. However it is done, the objective is simple: to assure protection to all migrant workers by banishing any uncertainty as to which social security law governs their obligations and their benefit rights in any contingency.

Maintenance of acquired rights

The third principle relating to migrant workers, the maintenance of their acquired rights, is also essential from the viewpoint of equity. Its importance, as with the first principle, is associated with trends in the development of modern social security legislation. In place of the idea of "personality" conferring title to benefit, many social security laws have substituted the idea of the "territoriality" of entitlement. This has the effect of restricting benefits to those people who reside within the borders of the country where the rights have been acquired. The development is the result of considerations which are as much related to the constitution of the country as to the basis of benefit rights and the financial organisation of the social security scheme.

In any case, the new developments have been matched by appropriate measures in favour of migrant workers. In the short-term contingencies a worker can obtain benefits in the normal way in the country of immigration; but the long-term contingencies involve very different consequences. In the case of invalidity workers cannot continue with their normal work in the foreign country; at the approach of old age they may be encouraged to return to their country of origin; and, if they die, the dependent members of their families could in certain circumstances be deprived of their means of subsistence.

In all these circumstances, any territorial condition placed on the right to benefit puts a limitation on the protection of migrant workers. This is all the more serious since the right to long-term benefits is often acquired at the cost of long periods of payment of contributions, of work or of residence. The principle of maintenance of acquired rights seeks to remove such territorial conditions so as to ensure to the workers concerned the long-term benefits which they have earned during the course of their working lives, even when they cease to live in the country in which they have worked. The precise methods of application vary in particular cases in accordance with the terms of agreements concluded between the governments concerned.

The principle of the maintenance of acquired rights is a logical complement of the principle of equality of treatment, ensuring for migrant workers not only a legal right but also an effective right to the same protection as that given to workers who have remained in their own country.

Maintenance of rights in course of acquisition

The fourth of the five principles relates to the maintenance of benefit rights in course of acquisition. In order to put migrant workers on a completely equal footing with their stay-at-home fellow workers, it is not sufficient to guarantee that the former will not lose such rights as they have already acquired. They must also be enabled to carry on acquiring normal rights to benefit, no matter how often they have been uprooted from one country to another in the course of their working lives.

The problem is that rights to benefit (apart from employment injury benefit) do not arise at a point in time; they do not depend upon the beneficiary being covered only at the critical date of the contingency. On the contrary, securing those rights depends on the completion of qualifying periods of contributions or employment or residence within the jurisdiction of the law concerned. The qualifying periods could be relatively brief for short-term benefits, but a matter of years for pensions, and they must be served.

In the absence of special measures, these qualifying periods would affect migrant workers adversely in two ways. Firstly, on moving from one country to another the migrant would have to begin afresh to serve new qualifying periods. Meanwhile the worker would be without any protection, despite perhaps having completed in one or more other countries the whole of the qualifying period required by the law of the new country. Secondly, as regards the longer qualifying periods, which may be 15 years or more for an old-age pension, it would be possible in an extreme case for a migrant worker to spend the whole of a working life in two or more countries with identical social security laws without completing the necessary period in any one of them. Such an employment history would not give the worker concerned any right to benefit, despite having been regularly and compulsorily insured under the laws in question and despite the various forms of financial contribution which such compulsory insurance might have cost. Even in less extreme cases migrant workers none the less run the risk of being entitled only to reduced benefit after a working life that would have ensured them complete protection if it had been spent either in a single country or in a number of countries whose laws demanded less by way of qualifying periods.

The way in which a social security reciprocal agreement commonly copes with the situation is interesting. The basic technique is simply to add together, as necessary, the qualifying periods served by the claimant, no matter which national law applied when they were served. A refinement of the rules is necessary where the various laws express the qualification differently: one law may speak of weeks of paid and credited contributions, or of paid-up quarters of insurance; another may require weeks or months of employment; or more simply years of residence; and the country's social security records will have been compiled accordingly. So the agreement must include conversion rules, or tables of equivalence, by which the claimant's life history of insurance/employment/residence may be standardised — first of all by the country which receives the claim, which is probably the one in which the claimant is living at the time. The technique enables the worker to satisfy the qualifying period for initial entitlement; and also fixes the rate of the benefit when this rate varies with the length of the qualifying period. A complete guarantee of rights in course of acquisition is thus achieved.

Finally, it remains to determine the law or laws to which reference must be made for purposes of benefit eligibility. Under the agreement this may be derived from one law only, that is to say, the law applicable at the time of the occurrence of the contingency, or the law of the country of residence of the person concerned; or it may be derived from two or more of the national laws involved, in proportion to the periods during which the worker was covered under each law. In the outcome, the claimant may acquire a partial entitlement to benefit under each national law, or a single entitlement backed by a financial adjustment between the countries involved. There are other technical methods which can be applied, according to the nature of the records which each country has maintained, but it is not necessary to go into them in this general discussion.

Payment of benefits abroad

The fifth principle, regarding the payment of benefits abroad, is becoming increasingly important in international relations in the social security field. Protection of migrant workers and their families cannot be achieved merely by the maintenance of existing rights. Such rights must be made effective by the payment of benefit in all cases where the special situation of the beneficiaries can reasonably be considered as a normal consequence of their being migrant workers.

The need to provide for payment of benefits abroad first became apparent in connection with old-age and associated pensions. More recently coverage has been progressively extended to include short-term benefits — in the case of sickness, maternity, employment injury and unemployment — and family benefits.

This removal of territorial conditions imposed by national laws is important to the workers themselves but still more to members of their families who may be living outside the country whose legislation applies. Furthermore, frontier workers, who by definition live in one country and work in another, may need protection, including medical care benefits, on similar terms in each country. Again, workers may sustain an employment injury outside the country under whose social security law they are insured and they must be certain of the protection provided by the law. More generally, if it is accepted that migrant workers who become unemployed ought to go back to the original country, or to another country where the chances of employment are more favourable, it is clear that they ought not to lose the help normally given to unemployed persons who are seeking new employment. Finally, it is frequently the case that workers who move to a new country leave a family behind, either because the move is a temporary one or because of the need to find necessary accommodation. In these circumstances they must not lose the right to family benefits and medical care benefit in the case of sickness and maternity. Other comparable situations call for special provisions which are to be found in the more complete instruments catering, for example, for workers or pensioners who fall sick or who are injured while on holiday abroad.

The various examples cited show clearly that the payment of short-term benefits abroad is of no less importance to the protection of migrant workers and their families than the maintenance of acquired rights to long-term benefits.

The methods of paying benefit abroad vary considerably with the nature of the schemes involved, the situation of the workers concerned and the particular branch of benefit. Moreover, the methods must take account of technical problems of administrative and perhaps medical supervision of beneficiaries who are otherwise outside the control of the institution paying the benefits.

Every reciprocal agreement is customarily supported by a separate instrument containing the administrative arrangements by which the responsible officials will exchange information for the purpose of putting the agreement into effect. This will set out in detail how payments are to be made; how funds are to be transmitted and accounted for; how the provision of medical care benefits should be organised; how the many services which a social security institution carries out for covered persons in its own country should be discharged on its behalf by the other parties to the reciprocal agreement; and how those extra or modified services which are dictated by the particular situation of the covered person abroad should be carried out.

The administrative arrangements drawn up by mutual agreement between officials of the States concerned, taking account especially of the size and direction of the migration of labour, can become elaborated into quite detailed procedural and financial provisions. But it is important to remember that these techniques all have the same objective: to give migrant workers and their families complete social security protection.

EXTENSION OF SCOPE

One particularly important development deserves to be noted: the extension of the five principles mentioned above to non-contributory benefits, which are largely or entirely financed out of public funds. Such benefits, which have traditionally been outside the application of some of the principles of international co-ordination because they are financed from national taxation, are increasingly being treated in the same way as contributory benefits. This development is inspired by ideals of social justice which take account of the fact that the effective participation of migrant workers in the financing of national social security programmes is not limited to those contributions which may be deducted from wages.

International agreements are also extending their application to a wider circle of covered persons. Just as national schemes of social security, from workmen's compensation onwards, concerned themselves first with particular categories of employed persons and gradually extended the scope of their protection, so the international co-ordination of social security laws began with special groups such as frontier workers, seasonal migrants and seafarers and spread to the broader scene of the movement across frontiers of employed persons generally. Because more countries are extending their own social security programmes to cover self-employed persons, the latest development that is to be seen in the most recently elaborated instruments is in the co-ordination of schemes as they apply to independent workers. At the same time, in many regions the barriers to free movement between countries are being relaxed. Thus, international co-ordination in the field of social security is developing and is being expanded to the same degree as the idea of social security is being extended by legislators themselves.

INTERNATIONAL AND MULTILATERAL CO-ORDINATION OF SOCIAL SECURITY

As early as 1919, when it adopted the Unemployment Convention (No. 2) at its First Session, the International Labour Conference provided that member States bound by the Convention who had established an unemployment insurance scheme must — under conditions to be laid down in a common agreement — make arrangements that would permit workers who were nationals of one State but working in the territory of another to receive benefits equal to those paid to workers who were nationals of the second State. Ever since then the Conference has consistently followed the same line, whether through specific provisions in the Conventions dealing with the various individual branches of social insurance, or through the special Conventions designed exclusively for the protection of foreigners and migrant workers which were mainly adopted before the Second World War. Among those Conventions were the Equality of Treatment (Accident Compensation) Convention, 1925 (No. 19), the Maintenance of Migrants' Pension Rights Convention, 1935 (No. 48), and the Migration for Employment Convention (Revised), 1949 (No. 97).

The ILO continued to practise this dual approach. Provisions relating to equality of treatment are found in the Conventions concerning particular branches of social security. In addition, there have been two new general Conventions: the Equality of Treatment (Social Security) Convention, 1962 (No. 118); and the Maintenance of Social Security Rights Convention, 1982 (No. 157), which revises the 1935 Convention and covers all branches of social security. The 1982 Convention is supplemented by the Maintenance of Social Security Rights Recommendation, 1983 (No. 167).

At the same time, the ILO has recognised the need to supplement its own Conventions, which are concerned with the statement of fundamental principles and the definition of general methods of co-ordination, with regional or subregional instruments aimed at co-ordinating the social security legislation of various groups of countries more closely and in greater detail. So a considerable number of multilateral instruments of co-ordination have been adopted with, successively, the Central Commission for Rhine Navigation, the Council of Europe, the European Communities, the Organisation of Central American States, the Common African and Mauritian Organisation and the Andean Group of Countries. In the case of the European member States, the work of the ILO in the field of multilateral co-ordination has gone beyond the framework of the European organisations themselves.

To make a fair evaluation of the remarkable development of international relations in the field of social security since the Second World War it is appropriate to recall that the multilateral instruments are themselves the result and the culmination of numerous bilateral agreements. While the origins of bilateral arrangements in the social security field date back to the beginning of the century, the multilateral arrangements which have been established under the auspices of the ILO, or with its technical co-operation, have developed particularly rapidly since 1950. Many factors have contributed to this growth. They include the general acceptance of the idea of social security, the setting up of subregional economic and political structures, the volume of migration by workers and, in particular, the organised migrations especially devoted to achieving economic integration.

The multilateral co-ordination of social security legislation has certain advantages over other methods. Firstly, it aims at achieving the equality of benefits which the persons concerned have the right to expect. Secondly, it assists in the work of the institutions charged with applying the agreements and, because of the considerable simplification of provisions and procedures that it permits, reduces their costs. Finally, the multilateral method is more easily adapted to the economic and political policies of whole regions which are moving towards a common constitution. Thus, this new phase of international relations has resulted in a rational division of functions between the laying down of fundamental principles of migrants' social rights at the international level and the co-ordination of social security legislations in as complete a fashion as possible at the regional or subregional level. At the latter level there has grown up, especially in Europe, a very effective collaboration between the various organisations concerned.

In participating actively in both of these movements, the ILO has honoured its original commitment to protect migrant workers in the field of social security and has held to its objective of being an instrument of social progress and co-ordinated economic development. Migrant workers are, as a class, particularly vulnerable in economic and social terms. Although social security cannot give them the complete protection that their overall situation demands, it is none the less an essential part of that protection and it is their due as a fundamental human right.

THE ROLE OF THE ILO IN SOCIAL SECURITY

16

THE ILO AND SOCIAL SECURITY

The opening chapter described briefly how the ILO prepares international labour Conventions and Recommendations which, after adoption by the member States at the International Labour Conference, stand as a code of guidance and advice and as a model for the formulation of national policies and for the preparation of national legislation on social security. Such instruments have been referred to frequently throughout the book and it has been shown how, without imposing uniformity in detail, they have moulded the shape and growth of social security programmes. In this chapter the Organisation itself and its various social security activities are examined.

The International Labour Organisation was established by the peace settlement in 1919, with a Constitution which brings together at the annual International Labour Conference tripartite delegations of its member States — workers, employers and governments, speaking freely with an equal voice on matters of common concern. These matters include, in the words of the Constitution, "the protection of the worker against sickness, disease and injury arising out of his employment . . . provision for old age and injury, protection of the interests of workers when employed in countries other than their own". Nowadays, the ILO takes a senior place amongst the specialised agencies which together are often referred to as "the United Nations family". The Conference of the Organisation elects a Governing Body, also constituted on a tripartite basis, and its affairs are carried into effect by the International Labour Office, with a headquarters in Geneva and regional and area offices around the world, under the guidance of the Director-General. The headquarters includes a Social Security Department and there are social security advisers on the staff of certain regional offices.

In 1919 only a few member States had social security schemes and these were mostly insurance-based. The development of the subject from then onwards falls into two main stages. The first, until 1939, was devoted largely to promoting the idea of workers' protection through social insurance. In the second stage, after 1944, the ILO broadened and diversified its view of social security. The new departure was marked by the adoption of the Income Security Recommendation, 1944 (No. 67). That document set out guiding principles and suggestions for their application in the several contingencies with which this handbook has been concerned, envisaging that income security should be organised as far as possible on the basis of compulsory social insurance; and that the maintenance of children and the needs of invalids, old people and others who did not come within the social insurance net should be provided for under social assistance arrangements. Accompanying this was the Medical Care Recommendation, 1944 (No. 69), which reached even further, proposing that medical care service should cover all members of the community, whether or not gainfully occupied, thus underlining the universal right of access to health services in an organised society.

Thus, there is a deliberative and decision-making organisation and there is a comprehensive set of principles. What means does the Organisation have of giving effect to these principles and translating them into action? The means vary from the setting of defined standards as targets for achievement — one outcome of an extensive programme of study and research — to practical technical assistance provided by field staff, and by other means, and the promotion of seminars and training courses in co-operation with national authorities and other international organisations.

THE SETTING OF STANDARDS

ILO standards on social security are contained, as for other subjects within the competence of the Organisation, in the text of Conventions adopted by the International Labour Conference. In effect, these set up targets which member States consider to be reasonable and attainable; they are to be brought to the notice of the legislatures; and, where national laws give effect to the standards, the States concerned may ratify the Convention and accept its provisions as binding upon them. The International Labour Office, by regular monitoring, encourages the whole procedure.

Although Recommendations have a persuasive effect upon member States, they are never binding. So the next action of the ILO, in relation to social security, was to refine and refashion the content of the Income Security Recommendation, 1944 (No. 67). The resulting instrument was adopted at the 35th Session of the International Labour Conference on 28 June 1952, as the Social Security (Minimum Standards) Convention (No. 102).

The year 1952 thus became a landmark in the work of the Organisation. Convention No. 102 was the culmination of more than

30 years of work and experience. It consolidated the previous international legislation and gave social security a unified, co-ordinated structure. Conventions before 1939 had confined themselves to a particular branch of the subject; the 1952 document is comprehensive, extending to the population at large and covering the full nine contingencies for benefit. States can, however, proceed to ratification without being bound to legislate for all the benefits. A certain order of priority is indicated but, broadly speaking, it is left to each State to build up its own programme according to its own needs and its stage of development. Moreover — and this was a novel departure, seen for the first time in a social security Convention — a developing country, "whose economy and medical facilities are insufficiently developed", could claim temporary exception from some of the more exacting, even if minimal, standards.

Having thus produced a broad framework of common standards to encourage the widest development of social security schemes, the ILO turned its attention again to the upgrading of standards for individual benefits within that framework. There followed the series of Conventions which are listed in Chapter 1 and referred to where appropriate in other chapters. These later Conventions may set somewhat higher standards in such aspects as the coverage of the population or the level of benefits, but the earlier, general, Convention remains in force to embody the basic minimum targets for each branch of benefit.

STUDIES AND RESEARCH

The elaboration of many national programmes of social security, and the continued demands placed upon them by society for extensions and adaptations and new assurances of automatic and genuine protection, are such that the search for improvement goes beyond routine changes, such as the adjustment of benefit rates, and increasingly extends across national boundaries. The development of international studies is therefore being pursued by the ILO in the knowledge that the comparative analysis of national experience must be particularly valuable to member States at a time when they have to reconsider or enlarge their own social security aims. The importance of ILO efforts in the field of social security studies and research is, if anything, increasing to meet the challenge of modern trends and the ever more important role which social security plays in the economy.

ILO research activity can conveniently be looked at under three heads: policy and standards, about which something has been said already; the examination in depth of particular subjects; and the preparation of training-oriented publications.

Policy and standards

The construction of an international standard in social security involves a tremendous amount of research work. The first step is to establish facts about the stage of development of social security systems throughout the world and to collect opinions expressed by experts from different economic systems and disciplines about desirable policies and about their adaptation and presentation in such a form as to meet the needs of countries at different stages of development.

Apart from the contribution which this fact-finding exercise makes to the formulation and improvement of international standards (culminating from time to time in the adoption of a new Convention or Recommendation), the process brings together ILO member States at regional conferences to discuss policy and promote the better development of social security protection. These, together with other lines of research by the ILO, have given rise to a series of reports about social security in particular regions. Major studies of this kind are used not only by the Social Security Department, and by the ILO in general, but have proven to be of great value outside the region and outside the circle of users for whom they were primarily prepared.

The more important social security laws and statutory regulations are regularly published in three languages in the *Legislative Series* of the ILO. In recent years this series of enactments has had to be selective because of the abundance of new texts arriving almost daily from member States. Further information about social security policy and legislative changes is published quarterly by the ILO in the *Social and Labour Bulletin*.

Specific subjects

The fluid nature of ILO research work, ranging from generalised comparison of systems to examination in depth of specialised social security subjects, is instanced by the regular publication of a variety of studies, such as *The cost of medical care* (Geneva, 1959), *L'impact macro-économique de la sécurité sociale* (Geneva, 1970), *Medical care systems* (Geneva, 1974), *Les systèmes de pensions dans les pays industrialisés* (Geneva, 1974), *Social security for the unemployed* (Geneva, 1976), *Social security in Africa: Trends, problems and prospects* (Geneva, 1976), *Social security for migrant workers* (Geneva, 1977), *Pensions and inflation* (Geneva, 1980) and *Financing social security: The options* (Geneva, 1984). Such studies are prepared either by the research staff of the ILO Social Security Department, or as specially commissioned projects by external consultants.

A major periodical publication which has attracted considerable interest is *The Cost of Social Security*. It first appeared in 1952 and each successive edition has reported the results of a survey of an increased number of countries. Its purpose is twofold: firstly, to provide a consolidated statement of the financial operations of schemes in both industrialised and developing countries, using a common working definition of social security and a uniform system of analysis; secondly, to provide an international comparison of the data by determining the trends in social security costs in various countries and looking at the distribution of the cost between different sources of revenue and between different techniques of providing benefit. In order to assess the importance of social security within the national economy, the data are also related to various national account aggregates such as gross national product or domestic consumption expenditure, either as aggregates or per head of the population.

The *International Labour Review*, published every two months by the ILO in Geneva, frequently contains legal and technical articles on major aspects of social security. The articles are based on specific studies of matters of current concern or of emerging importance to social security planners.

No less important than the material which is published for general information are the research and studies undertaken by the ILO to assist national governments in the integration of social security plans within the framework of their own economic and social development planning, and in meeting particular problems, such as the payment of pensions in rural areas, or the restructuring of a provident fund into a pension scheme.

Training-oriented publications

Training publications are designed for social security managers and administrative officials, although material of this kind may well interest a wider public. For example, the three volumes of the *Handbook of social insurance administration* (Geneva, ILO, 1962; mimeographed) provide detailed treatment of specialised subjects, aimed essentially at the training needs of developing countries, and the report of the training course held in Nairobi in 1980, *The ILO/Norway African regional training course for senior social security managers and administrative officials* (Geneva, 1982), has a value, and finds a market, outside the African region.

In the specialised field of actuarial practice, an important publication is P. Thullen's *Techniques actuarielles de la sécurité sociale* (Geneva, ILO, 2nd impression, 1974). This work deals with the whole body of actuarial techniques and systems of financing social security pension schemes. In addition, because of its theoretical as well as its practical aspects, the book is a most useful tool for training young actuaries and all those who wish to specialise in actuarial problems of social security.

Dissemination of information

The ILO has over the years of its existence accumulated an important body of documentation on social security throughout the world, compiled from official and unofficial publications and periodicals, through questionnaires and special surveys, through the reports and other information provided by the various regional, area and branch offices and national correspondents, and from information collected by the ILO experts and ILO officials on detached missions. This information is classified and analysed by the ILO staff and is continually drawn upon in response to requests received from every quarter.

WORKERS' EDUCATION

The pioneering work by trade unions on unemployment benefit was mentioned in Chapter 10 and the trade union movement has generally been much concerned with the development of social security policies and administration. Worker nominees serve on the boards of many social insurance schemes and provident funds and also on appellate bodies. The subject of social security has an important place in the curriculum of most workers' educational institutions. As well as being a subject in its own right, it features in training courses on economics, on wage negotiation (where so-called "fringe benefits" play a significant part) and on collective bargaining generally.

The Workers' Education Programme of the ILO is designed to help trade unions — in particular those in developing countries — to carry out their own education programmes. The Programme provides training materials, workers' education manuals and other publications in specialised series; advises organisers on such technical matters as course administration and curriculum development; arranges information and study fellowships for worker educators; and responds to requests for other kinds of assistance as they arise.

TECHNICAL CO-OPERATION

Together with its standard-setting activities, research work and continuous analysis and dissemination of information, the ILO has given practical assistance and advice to member States on the introduction or development of social security schemes. In the early years this usually meant short explanatory or advisory missions from the Geneva headquarters. These practical activities did not end in 1939. Even during the Second World War expert missions were sent to Ecuador and Mexico, Bolivia and Haiti, in connection with the planning of new social insurance legislation.

Sir William Beveridge consulted with the ILO during the preparation of his celebrated plan for the reshaping of social insurance and allied services in the United Kingdom. As the report,[1] published in 1942, says:

In order to be sure that, in making their survey, the Committee had the benefit of the experience of other nations, so far as it could be made available in the abnormal circumstances of the time, they sought the help of the International Labour Office. . . . It is appropriate that the Committee should express in warm terms their gratitude for the help thus afforded by the International Labour Office.

Since the Second World War the ILO has enlarged its technical assistance activities. This has been largely handled through United Nations channels, following the adoption by the General Assembly in 1949 of its "Expanded Programme of Technical Assistance", which harnessed the facilities of the UN itself and its specialised agencies, and the creation in 1965 of the "United Nations Development Programme" (UNDP).

United Nations Development Programme

The UNDP is administered under the general authority of the Economic and Social Council of the United Nations. It is financed by the voluntary contributions of governments belonging to the United Nations or the specialised agencies. All projects and programmes proposed for UNDP financial assistance must have the basic objective of promoting self-reliance in developing countries in respect of their managerial, technical, administrative and research capacity to draw up and carry out development policies and plans. The proposals must therefore conform to criteria which have been laid down by the General Assembly. Governments which ask for assistance — to be financed by UNDP and executed by the ILO or other specialised agencies — must show that they have, on the basis of priority needs, selected projects which will have a direct influence on the economic and social development of the country; are designed, whenever possible, for early transfer to the supervision and management of the recipient country; are integrated into overall national development efforts; are co-ordinated with other assistance programmes; and are free from political considerations.

Regular programme

Technical co-operation projects are not limited to those financed by the UNDP. The ILO has its own regular programme of technical co-operation. To be eligible for financing under this programme, a request must be submitted by a government or a group of governments, by a regional or intergovernmental organisation, or by employers' or workers' organisations in association with or through their governments. Any country may submit a request, but preference under the ILO regular programme is normally given to projects of short duration.

Multi-bilateral and trust funds

Some industrialised countries collaborate directly with the United Nations specialised agencies, including the ILO, to provide technical assistance. The allocations which they make in this kind of arrangement are known as multi-bilateral or "multi-bi" funds. Multi-bilateral projects are found in all the fields of competence of the ILO, including social security, and in some cases the agreement signed by the donor countries includes their assignment of associate experts to provide support for the ILO technical co-operation project.

Some countries, in order to avail themselves of the technical assistance facilities of the ILO, are prepared to meet the whole, or part, of the cost of a project by putting up the funds themselves, or by way of a loan from the World Bank. This then becomes a "Trust Fund" project. Whatever the source of the funds, the project is carried through at the technical level by the ILO in the same way that it would handle a project financed by the UNDP or under the regular programme.

OPERATING TECHNICAL ASSISTANCE

The ILO uses three principal methods of fulfilling its operational role in providing technical assistance:

(a) the assignment of experts, including regional advisers, to the country or countries concerned;

(b) the granting of fellowships for training;

(c) the organisation of regional seminars or training courses to enable the participants to study various aspects of social security with the help of international or national experts.

Expert advice

Short projects involving, for example, a preliminary or exploratory mission, or the giving of quick, high-level advice, are usually undertaken by staff members from headquarters or from the regional office. For longer projects, such as those financed by the UNDP, suitably qualified experts are recruited from outside the ILO. The job is difficult. Apart from technical qualifications, it calls for tact and diplomacy, a facility for quick adaptation to the very different conditions prevailing in developing countries and an appreciation that the methods and techniques used in the country from which the expert is drawn will not necessarily bring the required results elsewhere. Part of the difficulty is that, on social security missions, experts are almost always on individual assignments and, although briefed at the ILO headquarters and possibly also at the regional office, they are thrown very much on their own resources — a situation that most, but not all, experts thrive on. In the field they have the back-up support of the Social Security Department and other appropriate services of the ILO, as well as the Resident Representative of the UNDP.

Because of the tripartite basis of the ILO, contacts are arranged early on in the mission with representatives of workers and employers. Such meetings help the experts to familiarise themselves with local attitudes, needs and circumstances. Where there is a scheme in being, those organisations may be actively associated with its management and in any case they will be interested parties when the time comes to consider implementing any ILO proposals or recommendations arising from the experts' work. In all projects of a practical nature the host government is expected to nominate counterpart officers to work with the experts, in effect to be instructed by them and to carry on their work, or important aspects of it, when the mission is completed.

Not all technical assistance missions accomplish all that they set out to do, because it is only on the spot that the true scale of the task set, and its internal priorities and possibilities, become apparent. It can even happen that the expert's considered advice is that the plans are unrealistic or too ambitious in the state of development so far attained. In such a case the plans are not proceeded with. But most missions are successful, though some may take longer to come to fruition than was expected and some may produce positive results in a direction which was not envisaged at the outset.

The importance, to a social insurance scheme, of having professional actuarial advice when the scheme is being planned, and at regular intervals after it has gone into operation, has been described in Chapter 12. This is another variety of technical assistance provided by the ILO, either from the complement of actuaries in the Social Security Department or by recruiting actuarial expertise from outside.

Fellowships

ILO study fellowship programmes are used to aid young executives in developing countries to undertake periods of practical information or training in national administrations or in institutions responsible for the planning or administration of social security. Such fellowships are helpful, although they cannot replace the years of study — especially practical study — in techniques, management, the use of statistical data and the many other aspects which need to be mastered for an official in a developing country to become a competent, high-level executive in social security. The official is likely to benefit most of all from working side by side with an international expert undertaking a technical co-operation mission in the country, under the "counterpart" arrangement described above.

Seminars and training courses

The ILO has developed a specially valuable relationship with multi-bilateral agencies and governments in Scandinavian countries and some other industrialised countries. Funds have been made available to reorganise training courses and seminars at national and regional levels. The main aim of events such as these is to upgrade the technical skills of managers, administrative staff and other specialists in social security administrations in the region. Instruction is given, and discussions are led, not only by ILO technical staff and consultants but also increasingly by senior management staff from social security institutions within the region itself, whose practical experience lends additional authority to the event.

THE SCOPE OF TECHNICAL ASSISTANCE

So far, the machinery of technical co-operation between the ILO, the aid-giving agencies, the donor countries and the receiving countries has been considered. What, finally, is the technical content which the ILO is enabled, by those means, to bring to the receiving country? It can be categorised and set out as follows:

1. Co-operation in a general investigation into the economic, social and administrative situation of the country and in the establishment of an outline of a social security scheme consistent with present needs, administrative capacity and possible future development.

2. Drafting of specific social security legislation, including principal legislation and, where necessary, detailed regulations for the application of the scheme. This may be done either for new legislation or for revising or amending existing legislation.

3. Study of the problems of organisation and administration in a social security institution with a view to improving the operational techniques and procedures of the scheme. This may be generalised or may concentrate on specialised fields, such as accounting systems, the organisation of departments responsible for collecting, compiling and presenting statistics, the mechanisation of data processing departments or actuarial requirements.

4.   Study of the problems involved in providing medical care under a
      social security scheme.

CO-OPERATION WITH THE INTERNATIONAL
SOCIAL SECURITY ASSOCIATION

The International Social Security Association (ISSA) has maintained
close relations with the ILO ever since the Association was founded in
Brussels in 1927, under ILO auspices. Unlike the ILO, the ISSA is not an
association of member States but rather of practitioners in social security.
According to its Constitution, it groups together "services, institutions or
bodies administering one or more branches of social security or mutual
benefit schemes".

Originally a European organisation, the ISSA, with its headquarters
at the ILO in Geneva, now operates world-wide, having established
regional offices at Lomé (for Africa), Buenos Aires (for America) and New
Delhi (for Asia and Oceania). In June 1983 there were 330 members in 123
countries.

Every three years the ISSA holds its General Assembly, which
provides members with an opportunity to learn about and discuss the
general trends in the different branches of social security and its
administration.

The technical activities of the ISSA are carried out, at the centre,
principally through permanent technical committees dealing with:
—   medical care and sickness insurance;
—   insurance against employment accidents and occupational disease;
—   unemployment insurance and employment maintenance;
—   old-age, invalidity and survivors' insurance;
—   family benefit;
—   the prevention of occupational risks;
—   organisation and methods;
—   other subjects common to all branches, such as legal, actuarial and
      statistical questions.

Technical meetings and training courses are also organised at the
regional level, together with local research projects and the production of
regional publications.

The ISSA supplies its members with up-to-date information through
a number of periodical publications, most of them in several languages.
There are the *International Social Security Review* (quarterly), the *World
Bibliography of Social Security* (twice-yearly), *Current Research in Social
Security* (twice-yearly), and the *Automatic Data Processing Information
Bulletin* (three times a year). The Association has also built up a central
reference library of thousands of publications from all over the world. The

173

library is an invaluable source of information for the members of the Association, for interested laymen and for experts in the operation, promotion or development of social security.

CO-OPERATION WITH THE INTER-AMERICAN COMMITTEE ON SOCIAL SECURITY

The ILO continues to provide technical and financial support to the Inter-American Committee on Social Security (IACSS). Co-operation with IACSS has taken a new dimension since the adoption by the ILO in 1966 of the Ottawa Programme of Social Security Reform for the Americas. Established at the Eighth Conference of the American States Members of the ILO, this set out guidelines for the development, reform and improvement of social security in the American region. IACSS activities include an important training component — the Inter-American Centre for Social Security Studies — to which the ILO provides assistance and which is instrumental in achieving specific goals of the Ottawa Programme. The ILO, IACSS and ISSA are not alone in providing technical co-operation and organising research and meetings on social security in the American region. There are three other major organisations active in this field (Organisation of American States, the Pan American Health Organisation and the Ibero-American Social Security Organisation). It is therefore essential to ensure co-ordination and to avoid overlapping, so that the interested organisations can work together in their common effort to promote sound social security systems in the Americas. The Ottawa Programme gave the ILO the mandate to take the initiative in this respect — for example, bi-annual consultations are held under ILO sponsorship.

SOCIAL SECURITY ORGANISATION IN AFRICA

During the generation in which so many African States have become independent, there has been a growing and active interest in social security. The subject combines in an attractive way the ideals of social justice, the expression of national solidarity and aspects of practical economics, all of which are important to emergent and developing countries. It is an area (both technical and geographical) where the capacity of the ILO to give technical assistance can be deployed to good advantage, in co-operation with the various inter-African organisations which are finding strength in the still fluid economic, social, commercial and political scene.

For many years the ILO has been organising training for social security personnel in Africa, with the use of funds from the various sources which have been described: multi-bilateral sponsors have been notable in their support. African Governments have readily agreed to act as hosts for these events and the older-established social security institutions have taken part as consultants at the technical level.

At Abidjan in 1977 the Fifth African Regional Conference emphasised how important it is:

— that training programmes should be an integral part of the management of social security establishments; and

— that the ILO should assist and support the training not only of staff members but also of those workers' and employers' representatives who participate in the formulation and direction of policy through membership of statutory boards and advisory committees.

Since then both the ISSA and the ILO have intensified their efforts, but the need for training of senior social insurance officials is increasing and so is the need for co-ordination amongst those responsible for providing it.

Training — that is, management training — can be seen as a subject by itself, but it also combines with other ILO technical co-operation projects, such as actuarial studies, legislation, accounting and statistics, and is ultimately directed at the larger aims of achieving a greater harmonisation of social security systems throughout the continent and of obtaining a fairer protection for migrant workers and for other disadvantaged categories of workers functioning outside their national frontiers. All this challenges the development of increased practical co-operation between the ILO and the Organisation of African Unity (OAU), the Common African and Mauritian Organisation (OCAM) and other regional and subregional bodies.

Note

[1] Sir William Beveridge: *Social insurance and allied services*, Report presented to Parliament by Command of His Majesty, November 1942 (London, HMSO, 1942), para. 36.

APPENDICES

1. THE SOCIAL SECURITY (MINIMUM STANDARDS) CONVENTION, 1952 (NO. 102), OF THE ILO

This Appendix is included for information. Although dealing with all significant aspects of the Convention, it is not exhaustive. Persons who wish to find the precise terms of any matter dealt with here are referred to the wording of the Convention itself.[1]

General

The Social Security (Minimum Standards) Convention (No. 102), which was adopted by the International Labour Conference on 28 June 1952, defines the nine branches of social security benefit. These are:

(a) medical care;
(b) sickness benefit;
(c) unemployment benefit;
(d) old-age benefit;
(e) employment injury benefit;
(f) family benefit;
(g) maternity benefit;
(h) invalidity benefit; and
(i) survivors' benefit.

All but the first of these benefits are paid in cash, but two of them — employment injury and maternity — also include an element of medical care; family benefit may comprise a variety of components.

States which ratify the Convention, that is, which adopt its provisions into their national legislation, are expected to establish a minimum of three branches, including benefit for unemployment, or old age, or employment injury, or invalidity, or survivors. They are also to meet defined standards for the minimum coverage of their population, the minimum rates or amount of benefit and the minimum provision of medical care, where appropriate. The Convention requires, as a rule, equality of treatment for nationals and non-national residents; it sets out the circumstances in which benefit may be suspended and requires that claimants

177

and beneficiaries should have a right of appeal against the refusal of benefit. Other general provisions limit the extent to which employees (in an insurance-based scheme) or persons of small means should be obliged to finance their benefits by direct contributions or special taxation. These matters are set out more fully below.

Under the Convention, the State accepts general responsibility for the adminstration of social security; for securing and monitoring the financial soundness of social security funds; and for associating representatives of the protected persons, and employers, with the management of social security institutions where appropriate.

Minimum standards for coverage of protected persons

The standard minimum coverage required is as follows:

1. For sickness, unemployment, old-age, family and invalidity benefits, either:
    (a) prescribed classes amounting to 50 per cent of all employed persons; or
    (b) (except for unemployment benefit) prescribed classes of the working population, amounting to 20 per cent of all residents; or
    (c) where benefit is granted only subject to a means test, all residents whose means are within the limits prescribed.
2. For medical care, either:
    (a) all persons who could be covered for sickness benefit as in 1 (a) or 1 (b)
    (b) prescribed classes amounting to 50 per cent of all residents.
3. For employment injury benefit, all persons who are covered for sickness benefit as in 1 (a), plus death benefit cover for their wives and children.
4. For survivors' benefit, either:
    (a) the wives and children of all persons who are covered for sickness benefit as in 1 (a) or 1 (b); or
    (b) where benefit is granted only subject to a means test, all resident widows and children who have lost their breadwinner and whose means are within the limits prescribed.
5. For maternity benefit, all employed women who are covered for sickness benefit as in 1 (a) or 1 (b) and, for maternity medical benefit, the wives of employed or self-employed men who are so covered.

A State whose economy and medical facilities are insufficiently developed may, when ratifying the Convention, claim temporary exception from the standard minimum coverage. For the time being, it would undertake to cover at least 50 per cent of all employees in industrial workplaces employing 20 or more persons, including the appropriate element of cover for wives and children for medical care, maternity, survivors' and employment injury benefits.

Minimum standards for determining rates of benefit

The guidelines for determining the standard minimum rates of benefit are tied to a schedule of "standard beneficiaries" and "indicated percentages".

	Standard beneficiary	Indicated percentage
Sickness	Man with wife and two children	45
Unemployment	Man with wife and two children	45
Old age	Man with wife of pensionable age	40
Employment injury		
Incapacity for work	Man with wife and two children	50
Disablement	Man with wife and two children	50
Survivors	Widow with two children	40
Maternity	Woman	45
Invalidity	Man with wife and two children	40
Survivors	Widow with two children	40

Schedule

The schedule is applied in two situations:

1. It is applied where the rate of benefit is calculated by reference to the previous earnings of the beneficiary or covered person. The rate of benefit payable to a standard beneficiary, together with any family allowance involved, should be not less than the indicated percentage of the previous earnings plus family allowance. Formal rules should be prescribed for the calculation of the previous earnings. An upper limit may be set to the rate of benefit, or to the level of reckonable earnings. This level should not be set below the earnings of a skilled manual male employee (the Convention gives an earnings level "equal to 125 per cent of the average earnings of all the persons protected" as an alternative).

2. It is applied where benefits are at a flat rate. The rate of benefit payable to a standard beneficiary should (when any family allowance is included in each side of the comparison) be not less than the indicated percentage of the wage of a typical adult male labourer. The latter is defined as an unskilled labourer employed in the major group of economic activities with the largest workforce covered for the benefit.

In either situation, if earnings vary significantly by regions, it would be permissible to apply a different upper limit (for earnings-related benefit), or to determine a different standard flat rate, for different regions.

3. In a third situation (the public service or publicly financed benefit) the rate of benefit may be determined by taking into account the means of the beneficiary and his family, according to a prescribed scale. The prescribed rules should allow substantial amounts of the other means of the family to be disregarded before the scale rate of benefit is reduced. The total of benefit, and other means (if any) over and above the amount disregarded, should be comparable with benefit calculated elsewhere under the "flat-rate" formula.

Minimum standards for medical care

The minimum content of a medical care programme includes:

(a) general practitioner care, including home visits;

(b) specialist care in hospitals and similar institutions for in-patients and out-patients;

(c) essential pharmaceutical supplies;

(d) pre-natal, confinement and post-natal care by medical practitioners or qualified midwives; and

(e) hospitalisation where necessary.

In the maternity benefit branch, the medical care element should include items *(d)* and *(e)* of this list.

The standard minimum medical care element of employment injury benefit is more comprehensive, adding dental care, the provision of artificial limbs and other prostheses, the provision of eye-glasses and a wider range of specialist services. However, a developing country may, when ratifying the Convention, claim temporary exception from these minimum requirements, undertaking for the time being to provide in the employment injury branch only the general minimum medical care listed at *(a)*, *(b)*, *(c)* and *(e)* above.

Qualifying periods

For medical care, sickness, unemployment and maternity benefit, there may be imposed "such qualifying period as may be considered necessary to preclude abuse". According to circumstances, this qualifying period could apply to the husband (for maternity benefit) or the breadwinner (for medical care).

For family benefit, there may be a qualifying period of no more than three months of contributions or employment, or of one year of residence.

Standard rates of old-age benefit should be made available subject to a qualifying period of no more than 30 years of contributions or employment, or 20 years of residence. (A reduced rate should be secured after at least 15 years of contributions or employment.) Where a contributory scheme covers all employed and self-employed persons, there is an alternative formula — a prescribed average number of contributions over a prescribed period.

Similarly, standard rates of invalidity or survivors' benefit should be available after not more than 15 years of contributions or employment, or ten years of residence. (A reduced rate should be secured after at least five years of contributions or employment.) In the comprehensive contributory scheme, there is an alternative formula — a prescribed yearly average number of contributions over a period of three years.

Duration of benefit

Medical care and sickness benefit may be limited to 26 weeks on any one occasion, but medical care should, in any case, continue as long as sickness benefit remains in payment. Sickness benefit may be withheld for the first three (waiting) days. A developing country may, on ratifying the Convention, claim a temporary dispensation to limit the duration to 13 weeks on any one occasion.

Unemployment benefit may be limited, where classes of employees are covered, to 13 weeks in any 12 months; or, where residents are covered subject to a means test, to 26 weeks in any 12 months. Up to seven waiting days may be imposed.

Maternity cash benefits may be limited to 12 weeks, unless a longer period of abstention from work is required or authorised by national laws — in which case, benefit shall continue throughout the period of abstention.

Other benefits are payable for the duration of the contingency, except that three waiting days may be imposed on employment injury benefits and invalidity benefit may be superseded by old-age benefit at pensionable age.

Miscellaneous matters

1. In general, non-national residents should have the same rights as national residents, but:

   (a) where benefits are payable wholly or mainly from public funds, special qualifying rules may apply to persons who were born outside the territory; and

   (b) where benefits are payable under a social insurance scheme, the rights of the nationals of another country may be subjected to the terms of a reciprocal agreement between the countries concerned.

2. Benefits under various branches may be suspended:

   (a) during absence abroad;

   (b) while a person is maintained at public expense in an institution (but any excess over the cost of maintenance should be paid to dependants);

   (c) if a person is simultaneously entitled to two forms of cash benefit — other than family benefit (he should receive not less than the amount of the larger of the two conflicting benefits);

   (d) where the contingency was caused by wilful misconduct or criminal offence on the part of the claimant, or the claim was fraudulent;

   (e) where a person neglects to make use of medical or rehabilitation services, or fails to observe prescribed rules of behaviour during the contingency;

   (f) in the case of unemployment benefit, where the claimant neglects to make use of the employment services, or lost his job as the result of a trade dispute, or left the job voluntarily without just cause; or

   (g) in the case of survivors' benefit, where a widow is living with a man as his wife.

3. Claimants should have a right of appeal against the refusal of benefit, or in respect of its quality or quantity but, where medical care services are provided by a government department, complaints in that respect are to be referred to the appropriate authority.

4. The cost of benefits and administration is to be borne collectively in such a way that:

   (a) hardship to persons of small means is avoided;

   (b) the economic situation of the country, and of the classes of persons protected, is taken into account; and

   (c) in branches covered by social insurance arrangements (and excluding family benefit, and, normally, employment injury), the total of the employees' contributions should not exceed 50 per cent of the total cost.

5. The Convention does not apply to seafarers and seafishermen, who have their own Social Security (Seafarers) Convention, 1946 (No. 70), and Seafarers' Pensions Convention, 1946 (No. 71).

2. SUGGESTIONS FOR FURTHER READING

Publications of the International Labour Office

Unemployment insurance schemes, Studies and Reports, New Series, No. 42 (Geneva, 1955), 254 pp.

Revision of Conventions Nos. 35, 36, 37, 38, 39 and 40 concerning Old-Age, Invalidity and Survivors' Pensions, Report V, Part 1, International Labour Conference, 50th Session (Geneva, 1966), 107 pp.

Revision of Conventions Nos. 24 and 25 concerning Sickness Insurance, Report VI, Part 1, International Labour Conference, 52nd Session (Geneva, 1968), 80 pp.

Robert Savy: *Social security in agriculture and rural areas*, Studies and Reports, New Series, No. 78 (Geneva, 1972), 268 pp.

Derick H. Fulcher: *Medical care systems: Public and private health insurance in selected industrialised countries* (Geneva, 1974), 178 pp.

Jacques Doublet: *L'aide aux familles: Contribution de la sécurité sociale à la politique démographique* (Geneva, 1975).

Pierre Mouton: *Social security in Africa: Trends, problems and prospects* (Geneva, 1976), 166 pp.

Social security for the unemployed (Geneva, 1976), 70 pp.

Social security for migrant workers (Geneva, 1977), 154 pp.

Social security for teachers (Geneva, 1979), 46 pp.

Pensions and inflation: An international discussion (Geneva, 2nd impression, 1980), 136 pp.

The Cost of Social Security: Tenth International Inquiry, 1975-1977 (Geneva, 1981), 115 pp.

Constitution of the International Labour Organisation and Standing Orders of the International Labour Conference (Geneva, 1982), 84 pp.

The ILO/Norway African regional training course for senior social security managers and administrative officials (Geneva, 1982), 333 pp.

Maintenance of rights in social security, Report V, International Labour Conference, 69th Session (Geneva, 1983), 101 pp.

Social aspects of industrialisation, Report VII, International Labour Conference, 69th Session (Geneva, 1983), 135 pp.

Financing social security: The options (Geneva, 1984).

Into the twenty-first century: The development of social security (Geneva, 1984).

Publications of the International Social Security Association

The following list includes reports on specialised conferences and meetings organised by the ISSA, as well as a number of studies carried out by the Association as part of its research programme.

No. 2. *The planning of social security* (Geneva, 1971), 208 pp.

No. 3. *Complementary pension institutes or complementary pension schemes* (Geneva, 1973), 243 pp.

No. 4. *Current issues in social security planning: Concepts and techniques* (Geneva, 1973), 183 pp.

No. 5. *Women and social security* (Geneva, 1973), 288 pp.

No. 6. *The role of social services in social security: Trends and perspectives* (Geneva, 1974), 181 pp.

No. 7. Lucien Féraud: *Complementary pensions: A comparative analysis* (Geneva, 1975), 145 pp.

No. 8. *Methods of evaluating the effectiveness of social security programmes* (Geneva, 1976), 160 pp.

No. 9. *Implications for social security of research on aging and retirement* (Geneva, 1977), 88 pp.

No. 10. *Problems of social security under economic recession and inflation* (Geneva, 1978), 112 pp.

No. 11. *Social security provisions in case of divorce* (Geneva, 1978), 128 pp.

No. 12. *Social protection for the over-75s* (Geneva, 1979), 85 pp.

No. 13. *Social security and taxation* (Geneva, 1979), 163 pp.

No. 14. Martin Tracy: *Retirement age practices in ten industrial societies, 1960-1976* (Geneva, 1979), 170 pp.

No. 15. *Methods of financing social security* (Geneva, 1979), 111 pp.

No. 16. *Absenteeism and social security* (Geneva, 1981), 175 pp.

No. 17. *Social security and disability: Issues in policy research* (Geneva, 1981), 185 pp.

No. 18. *Medical care under social security in developing countries* (Geneva, 1982), 170 pp.

No. 19. *Improving cost-effectiveness in health care* (Geneva, 1983), 173 pp.

No. 20. *The teaching of social security* (includes extensive bibliographies of source material used in Australia, the United Kingdom, the United States and the USSR) (Geneva, 1983), 135 pp.

Other publications

Everett M. Kassalow: *The role of social security in economic development*, United States Department of Health and Human Services, Social Security Administration (Washington, DC, Government Printing Office, 1968).

C. A. Oram: *Social policy and administration in New Zealand* (Wellington, New Zealand University Press, 1969).

Personal health care and social security, Report of a joint ILO/WHO Committee (Geneva, World Health Organisation, 1971).

Philip Booth: *Social security in America* (Ann Arbor (Michigan), University of Michigan and Wayne State University, 1973).

Measuring disability, Occasional Reports on Social Administration, No. 54 (London, George Bell and Sons, 1974).

Complementary systems of social security, 1973 Yearbook of the European Institute of Social Security, Parts II and III (Brussels, Aurelia Books, 1975).

Brian Abel-Smith: *Value for money in health services*, a comparative study (London, Heinemann, 1976).

David E. Woodsworth: *Social security and national policy, Sweden, Yugoslavia and Japan* (Montreal and London, McGill Queen's University Press, 1977).

Saul J. Blaustein and Isabel Craig: *An international review of unemployment insurance schemes* (Kalamazoo (Michigan), W. E. Upjohn Institute for Employment Research, 1977).

Pension funds in the United Kingdom, Economist Intelligence Unit, Special Report, No. 43 (London, Economist Intelligence Unit, 1977).

Leslie D. McClements: *The economics of social security* (London, Heinemann, 1978).

The social security retirement test: Right or wrong? (Washington, DC, American Enterprise Institute, 1978).

The tax/benefit position of selected income groups in OECD member countries in 1971-76 (Paris, OECD, 1978).

Sheila B. Kamerman and Alfred J. Kahn (eds.): *Family policy (government and families in fourteen countries)* (New York, Columbia University Press, 1978).

Dorothy Wilson: *The welfare state in Sweden: A study in comparative social administration* (London, Heinemann, 1979).

J. Gough: *The political economy of the welfare state* (London, Macmillan, 1979).

Social security and the redistribution of income, 1974-1977 Yearbook of the European Institute of Social Security, Part I (Deventer (Netherlands), Kluwer, 1979).

Social security reforms in Europe, 1978-80 Yearbook of the European Institute of Social Security, Part II (Deventer (Netherlands), Kluwer, 1980).

Enrique Lombera: *Social security in the process of industrial change: From the industrial revolution to the present day* (Mexico, Instituto Mexicano de Seguro Social, 1980).

Guide to pension schemes (London, Incomes Data Services Ltd., 1980), 90 pp.

T. H. Kewley: *Australian social security today* (Sydney, Sydney University Press, 1980).

TUC guide to occupational pension schemes (London, Trades Union Congress, 1981).

J. Higgins: *States of welfare: Comparative analysis in social* policy (Oxford, B. Blackwell and M. Robertson, 1981).

P. Flora and A. J. Heidenheimer: *The development of welfare states in Europe and America* (New Brunswick, Transition Books, 1981).

Peter A. Köhler and Hans F. Zacher (ed.) in collaboration with Martin Partington: *The evolution of social insurance 1881-1981: Studies of Germany, France, Great Britain, Austria and Switzerland*, Max Planck Institute for Foreign and International Social Law (London, Francis Pinter, 1982, and New York, St. Martin's Press, 1982).

Sara E. Rix and Paul Fisher: *Retirement-age policy: An international perspective* (New York, Pergamon Press, 1982).

United States Department of Health and Human Services, Social Security Administration: *Social security programs throughout the world, 1981*, Research Report, No. 58 (Washington, DC, Government Printing Office, 1982).

Note

[1] See ILO: *International Labour Conventions and Recommendations, 1919-1981* (Geneva, 1982).